AF486062

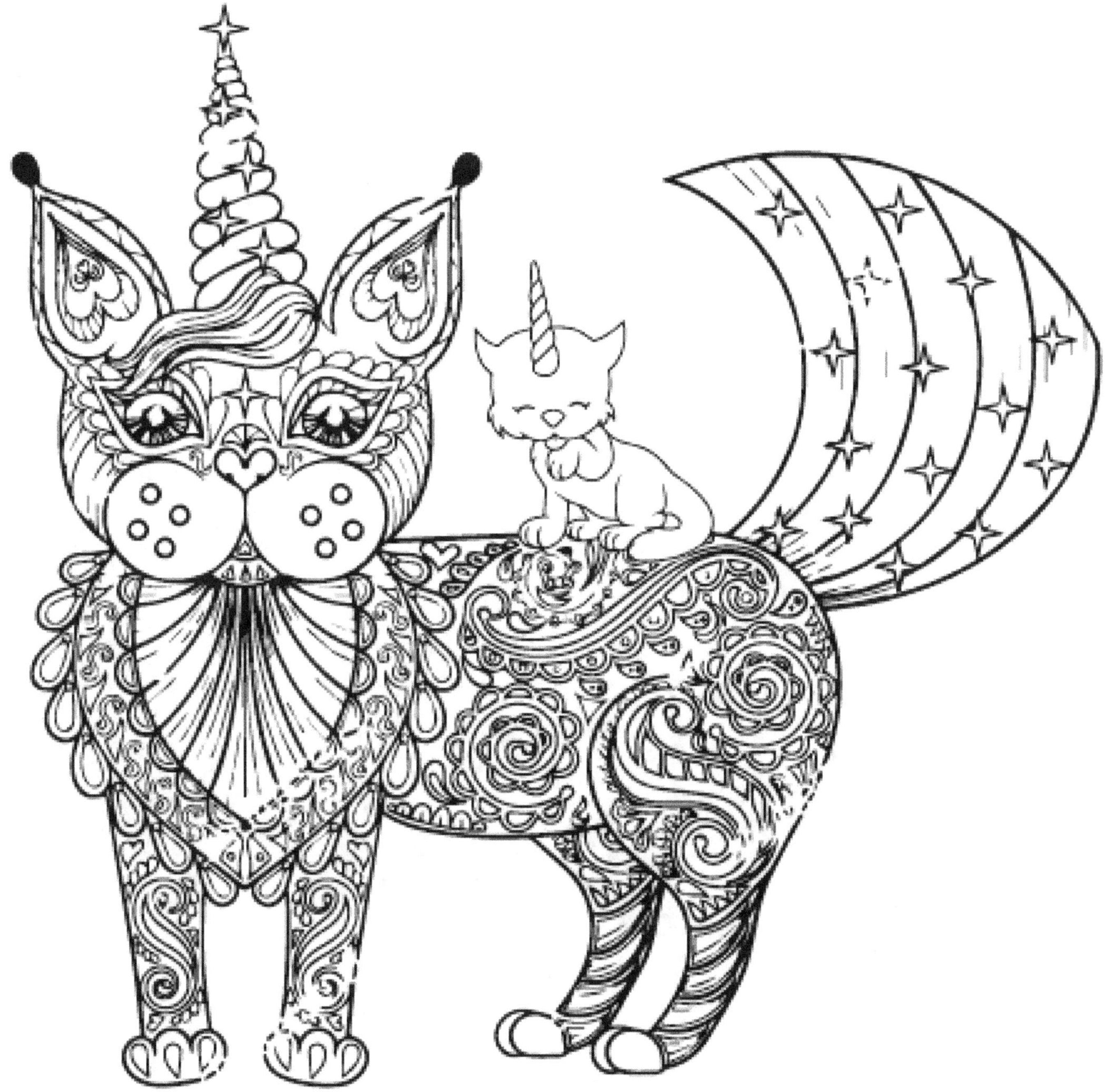

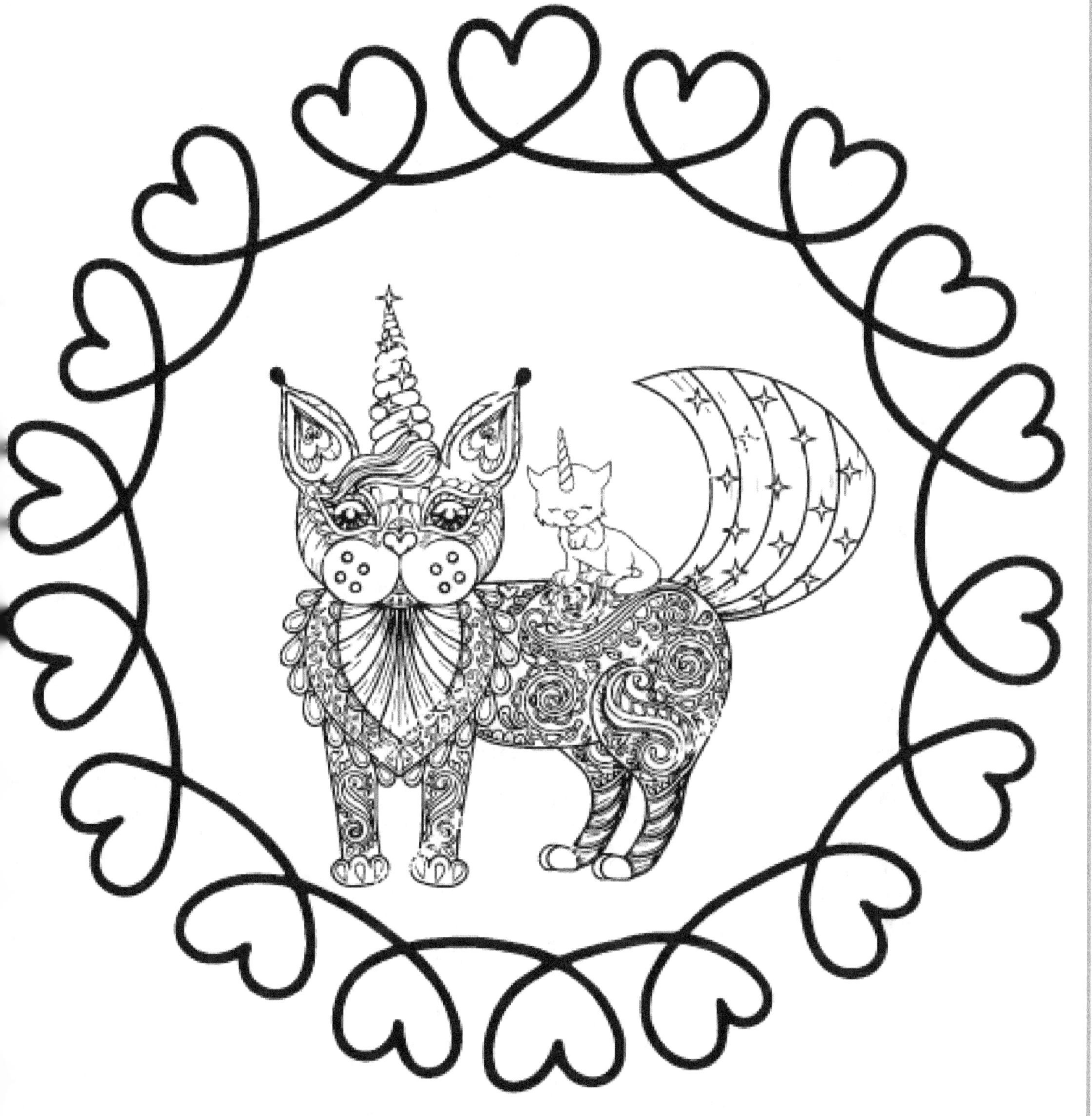

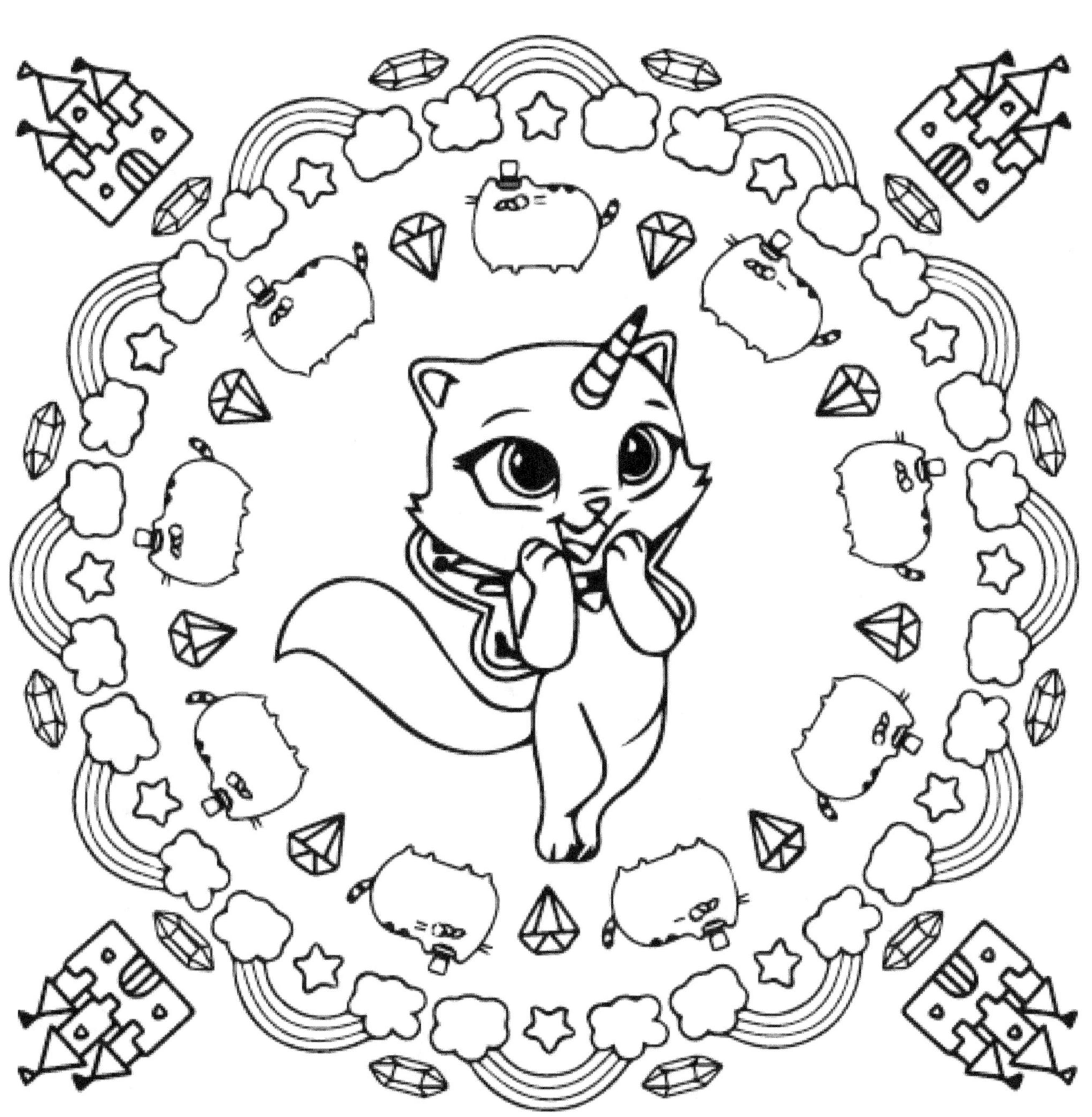

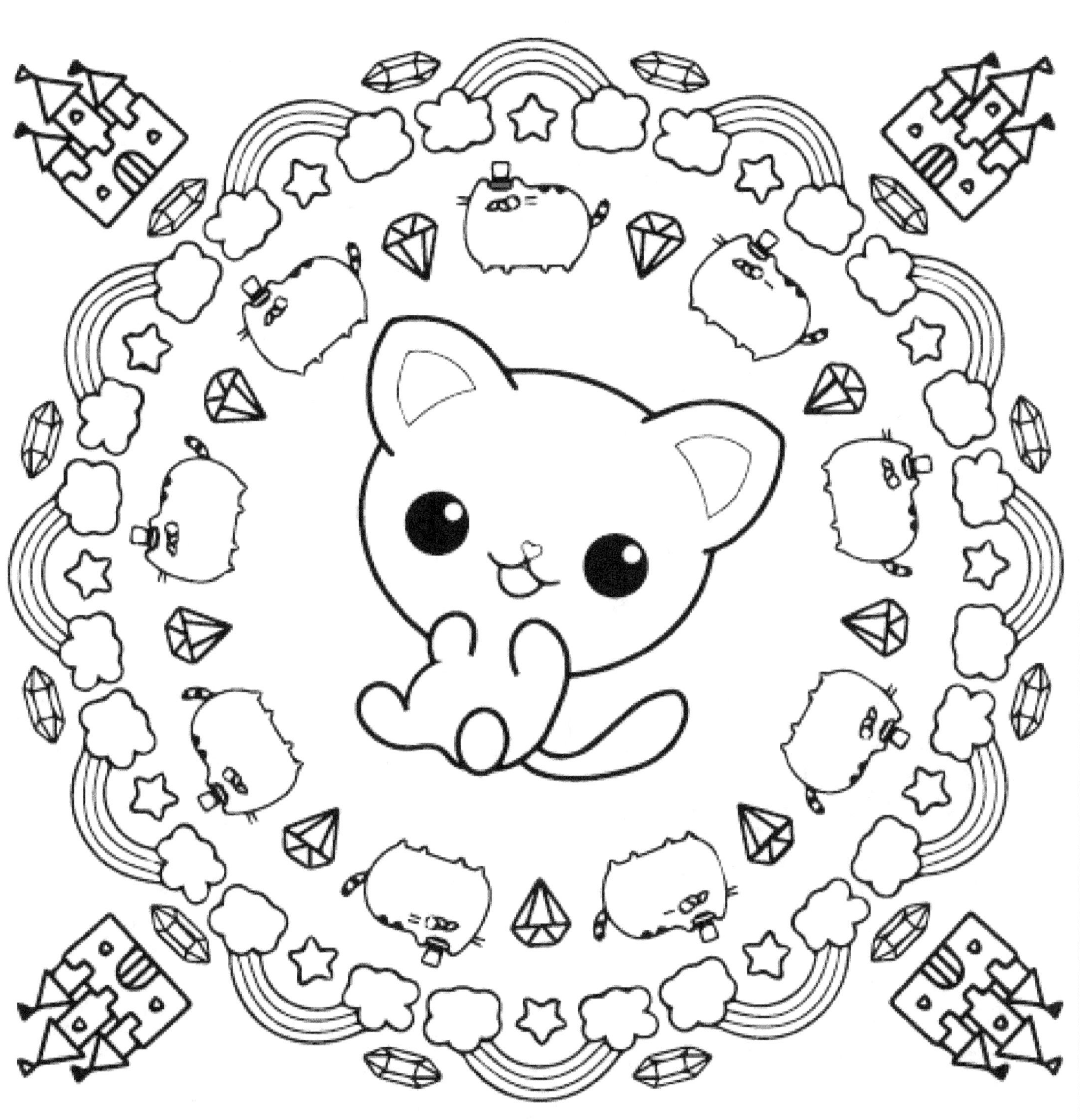

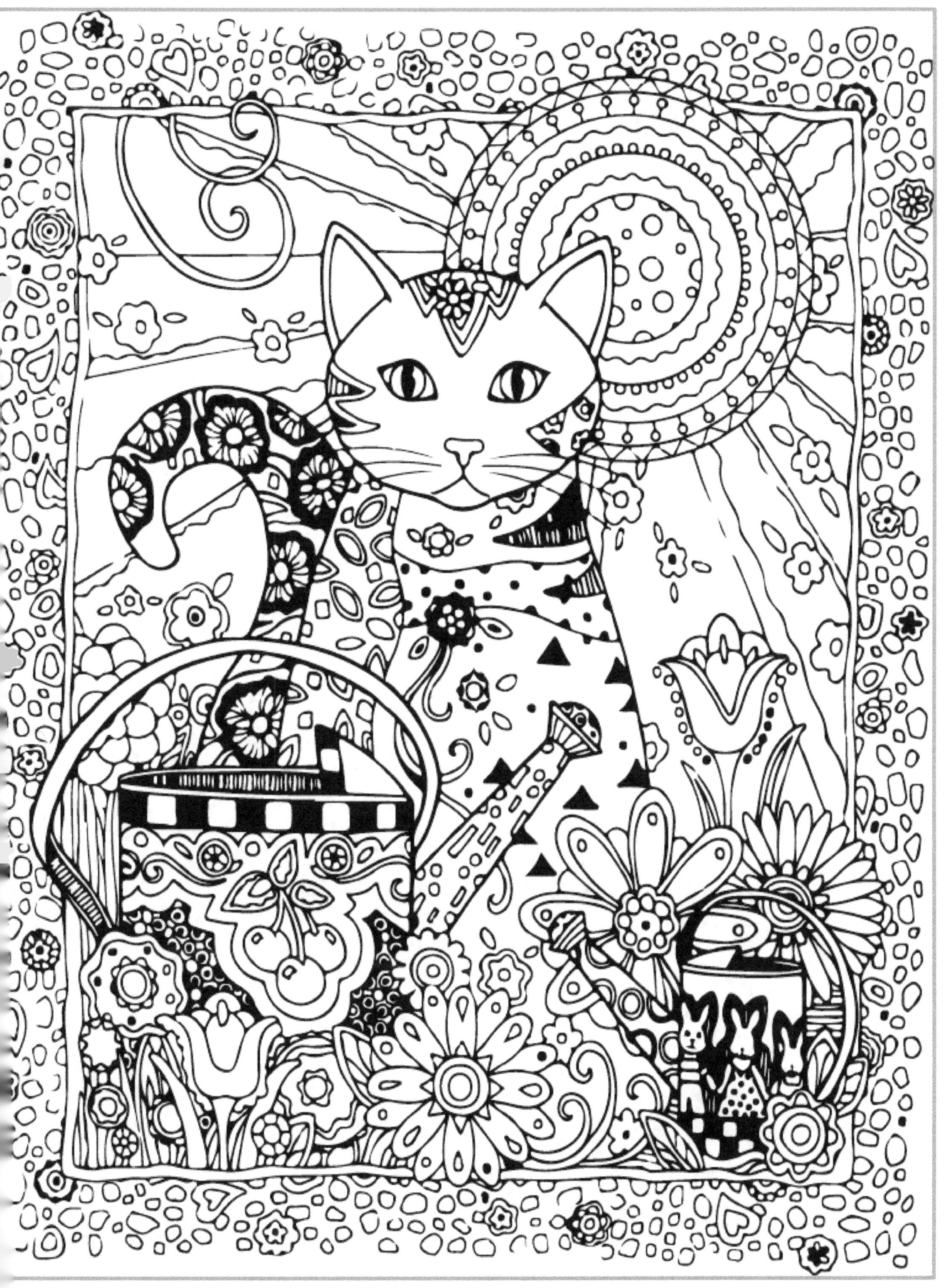

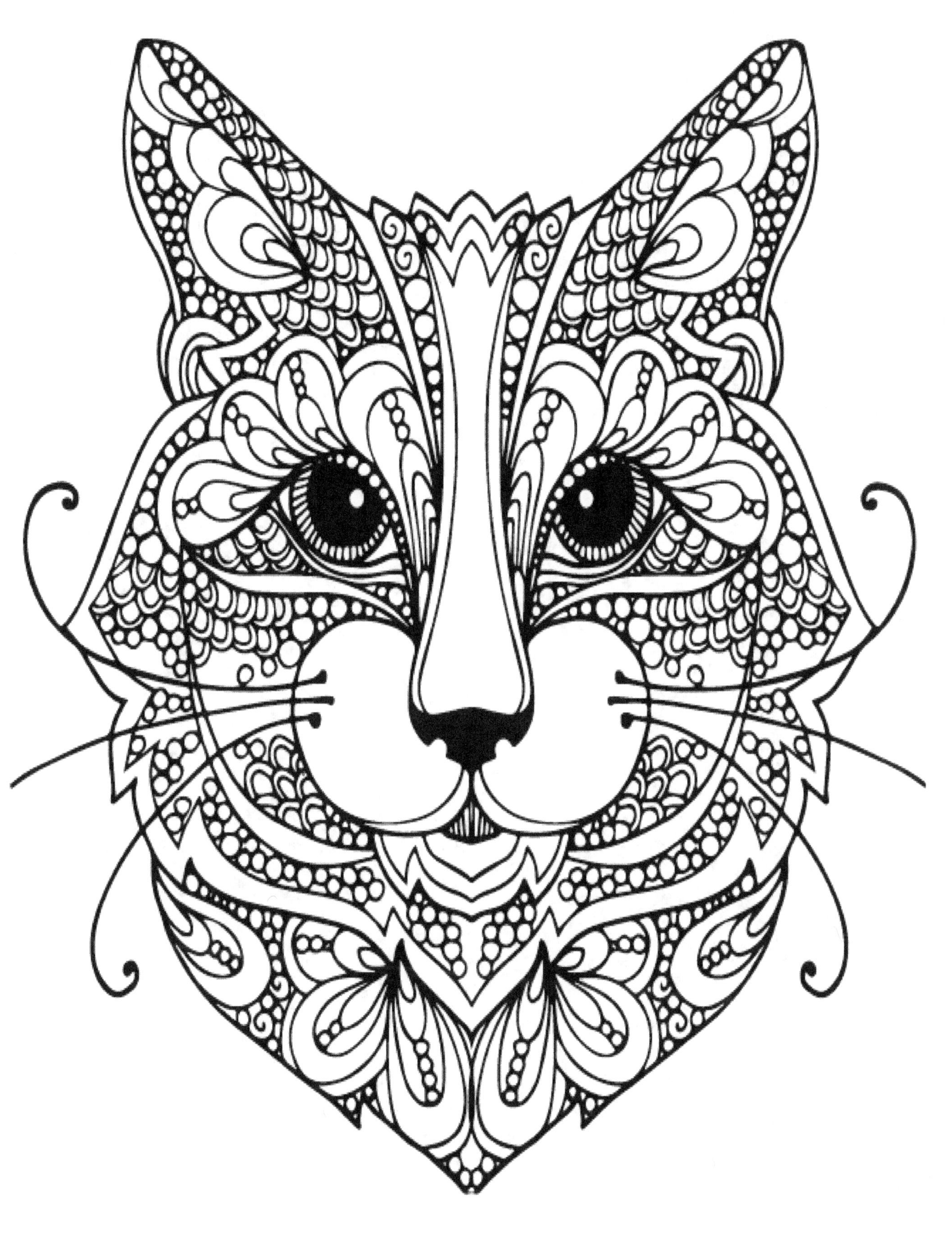

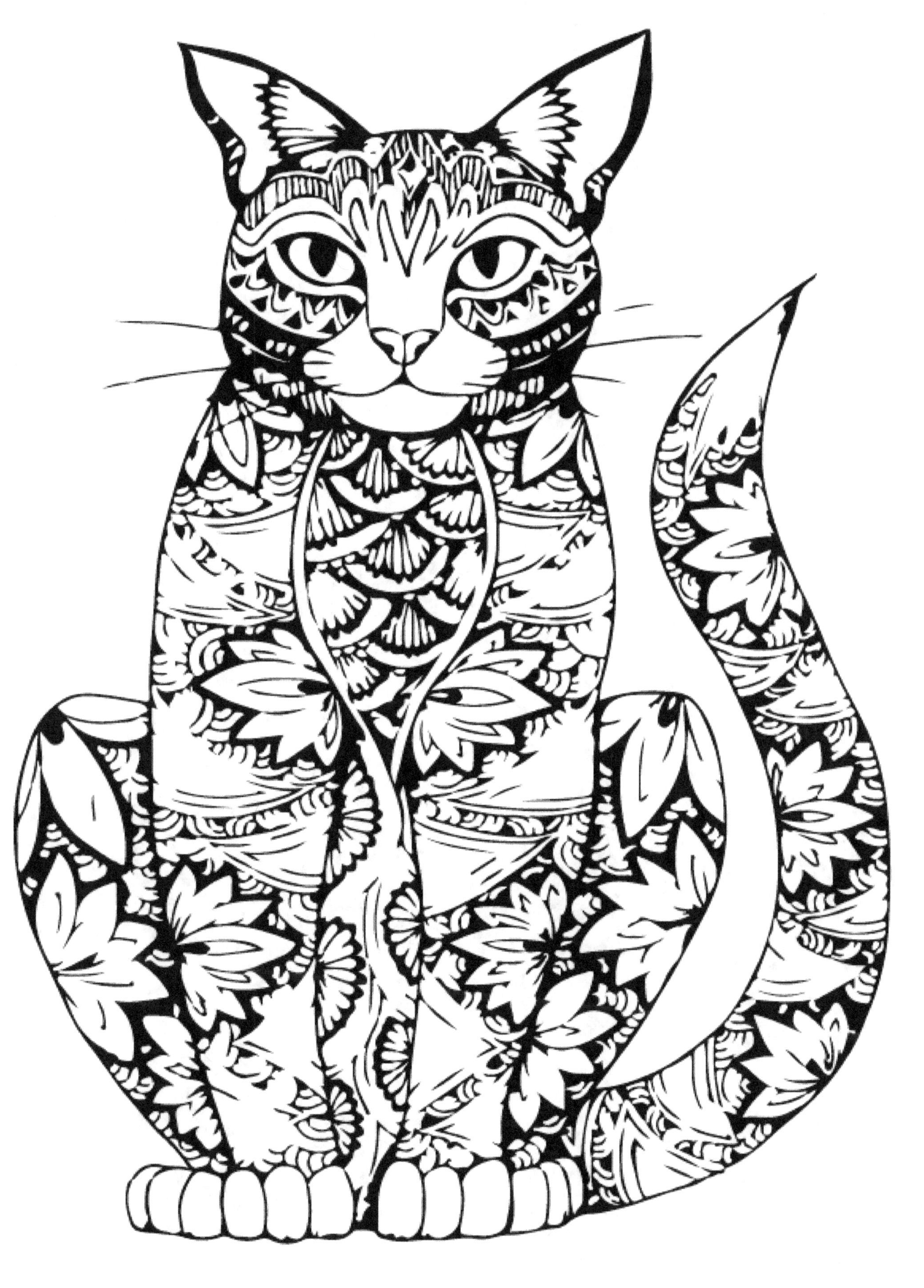

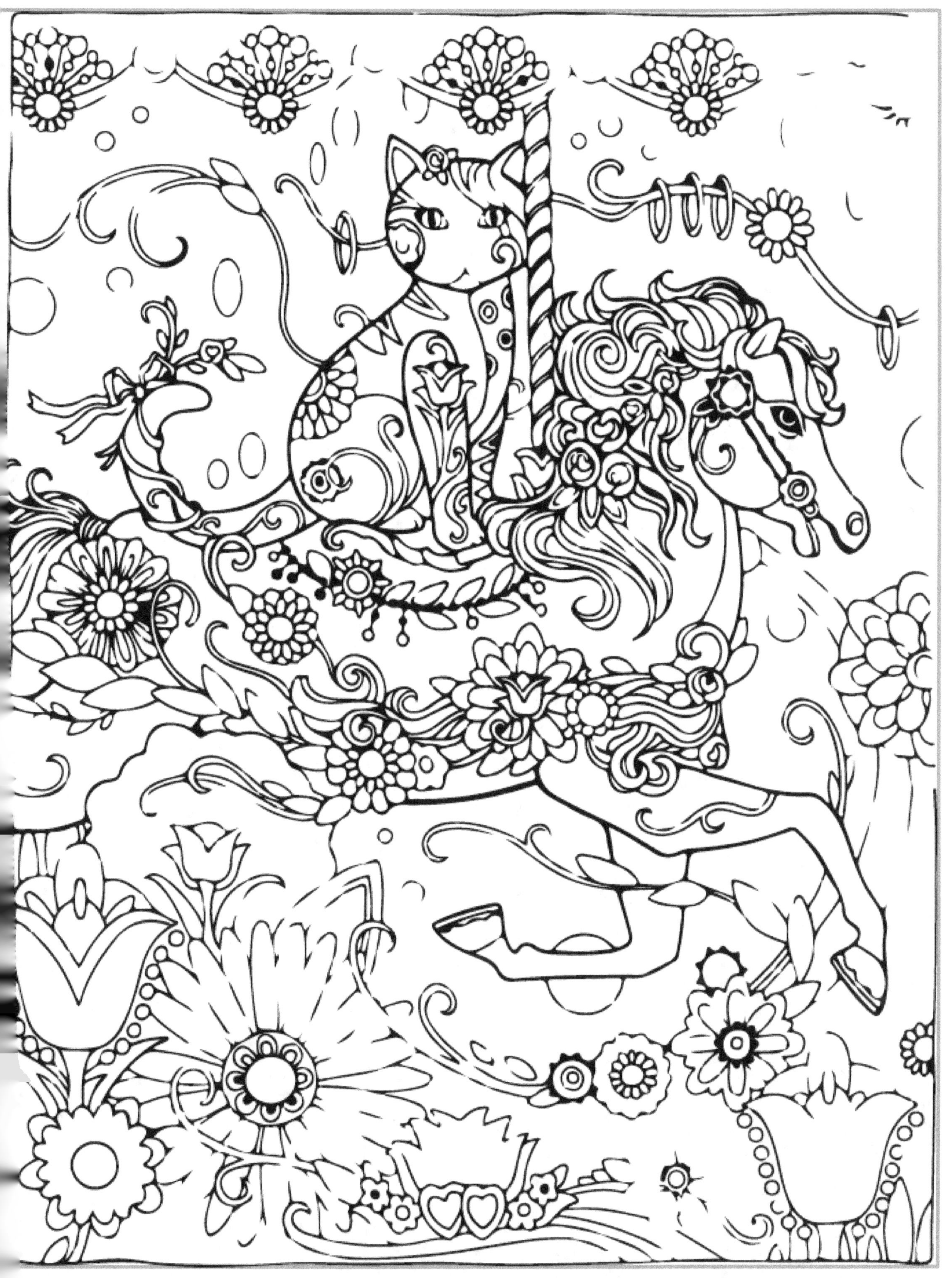

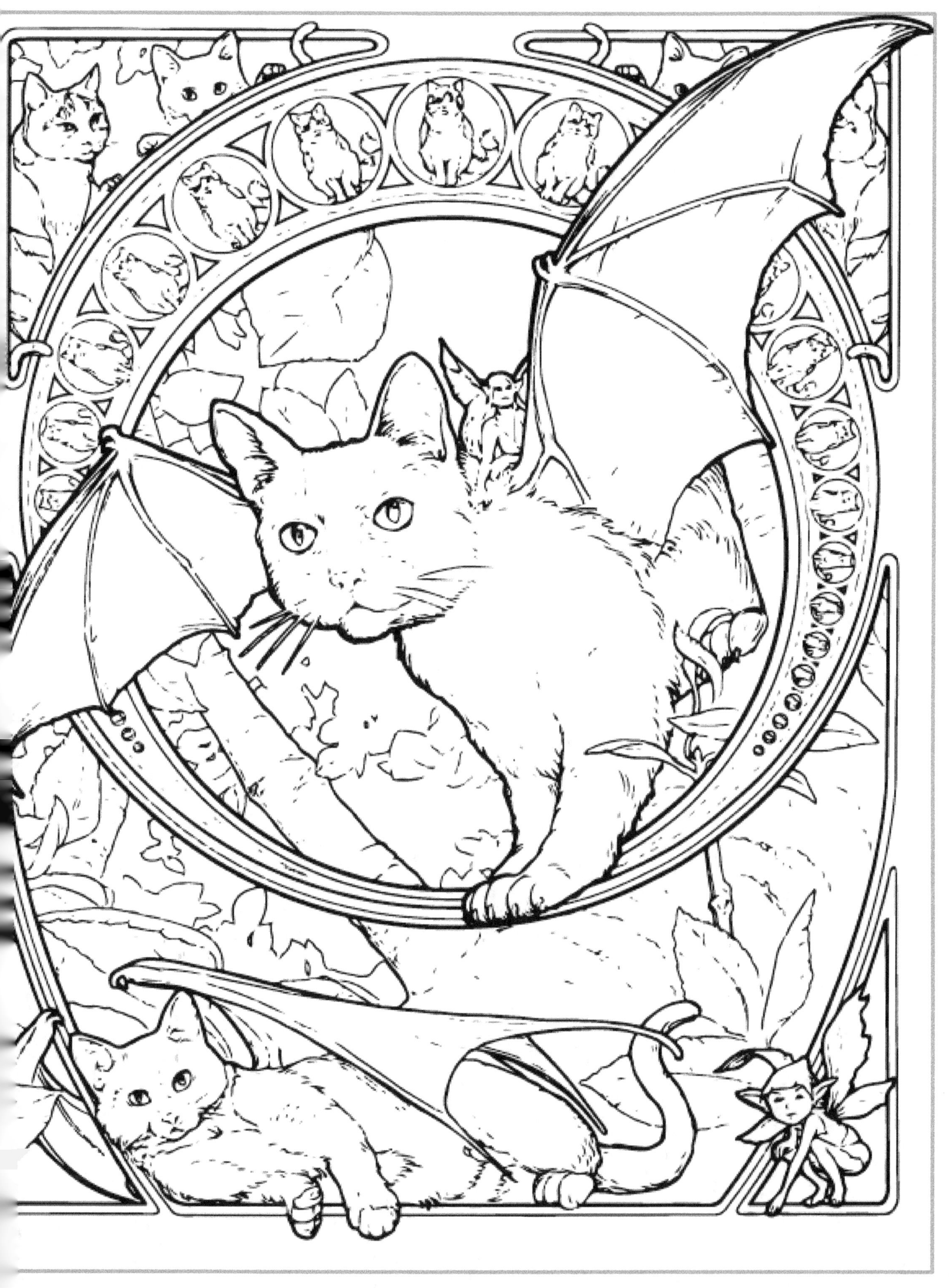

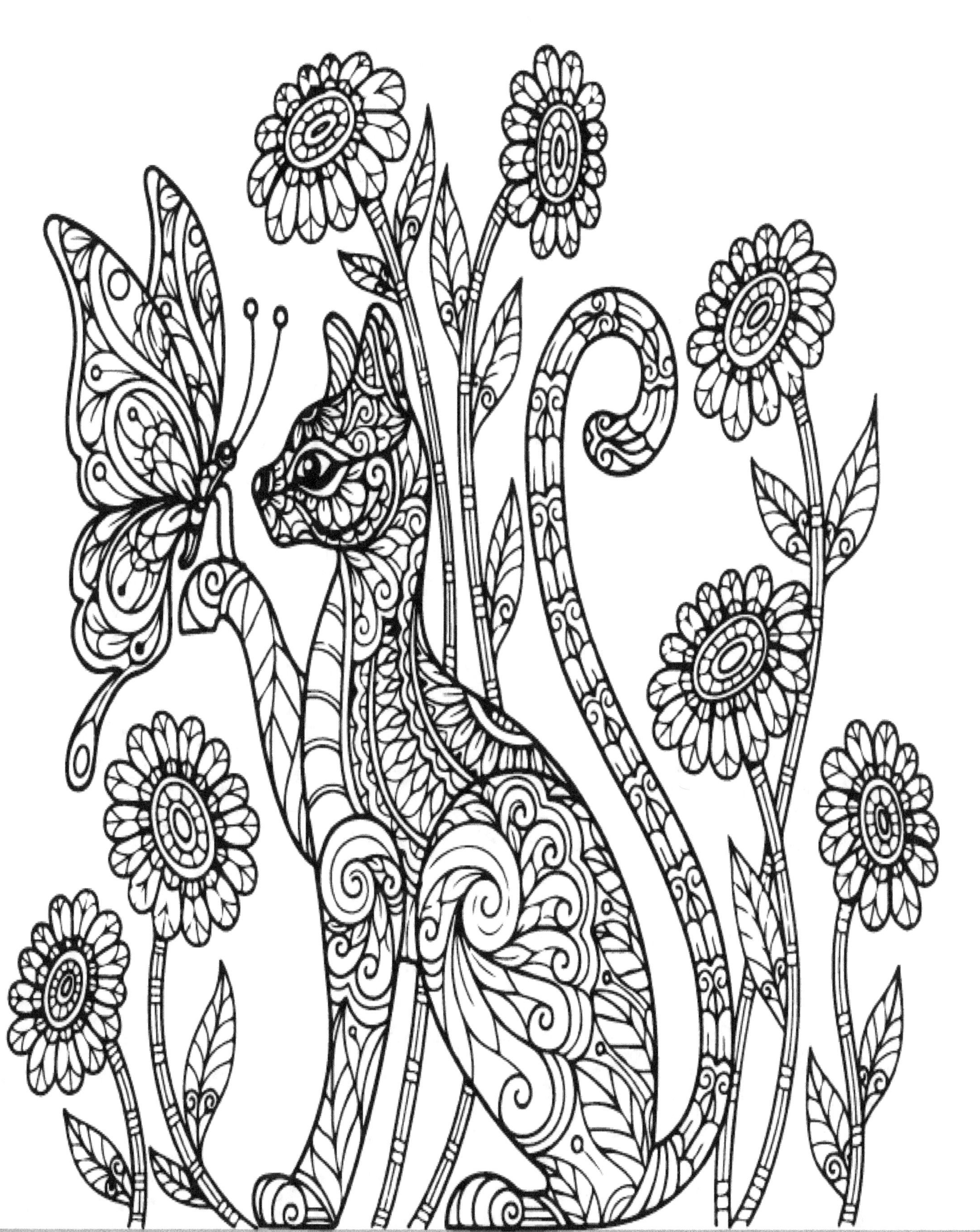

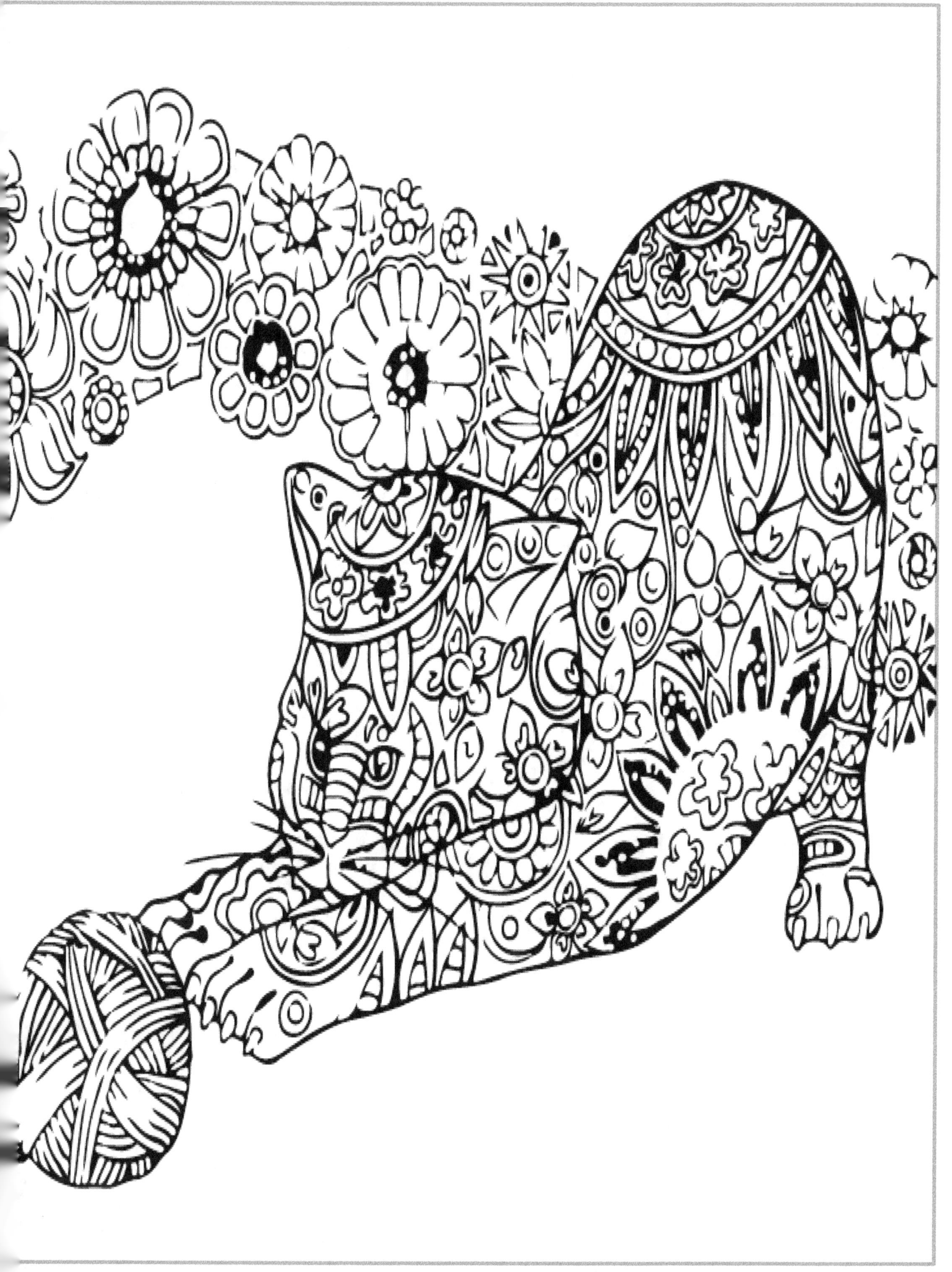

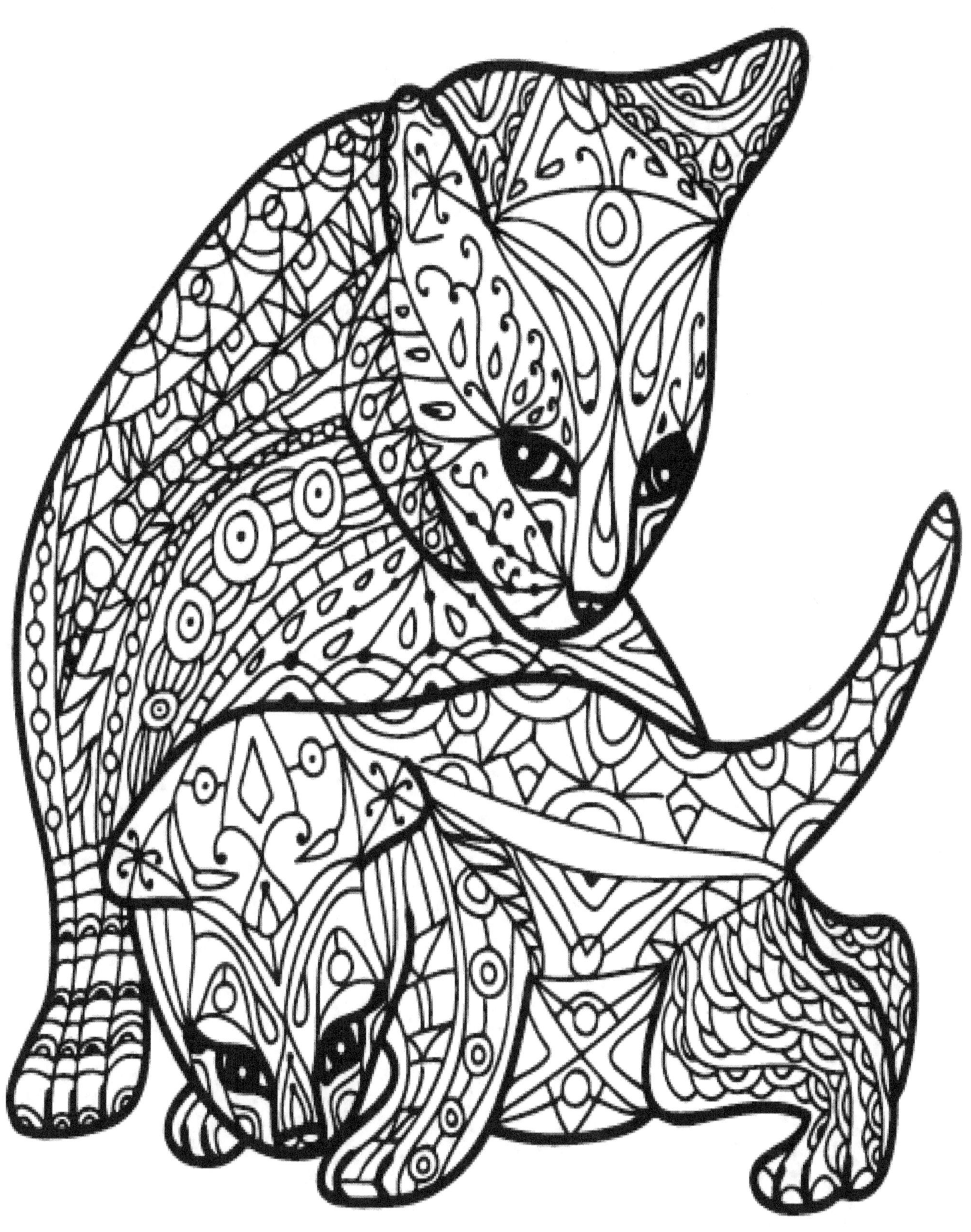

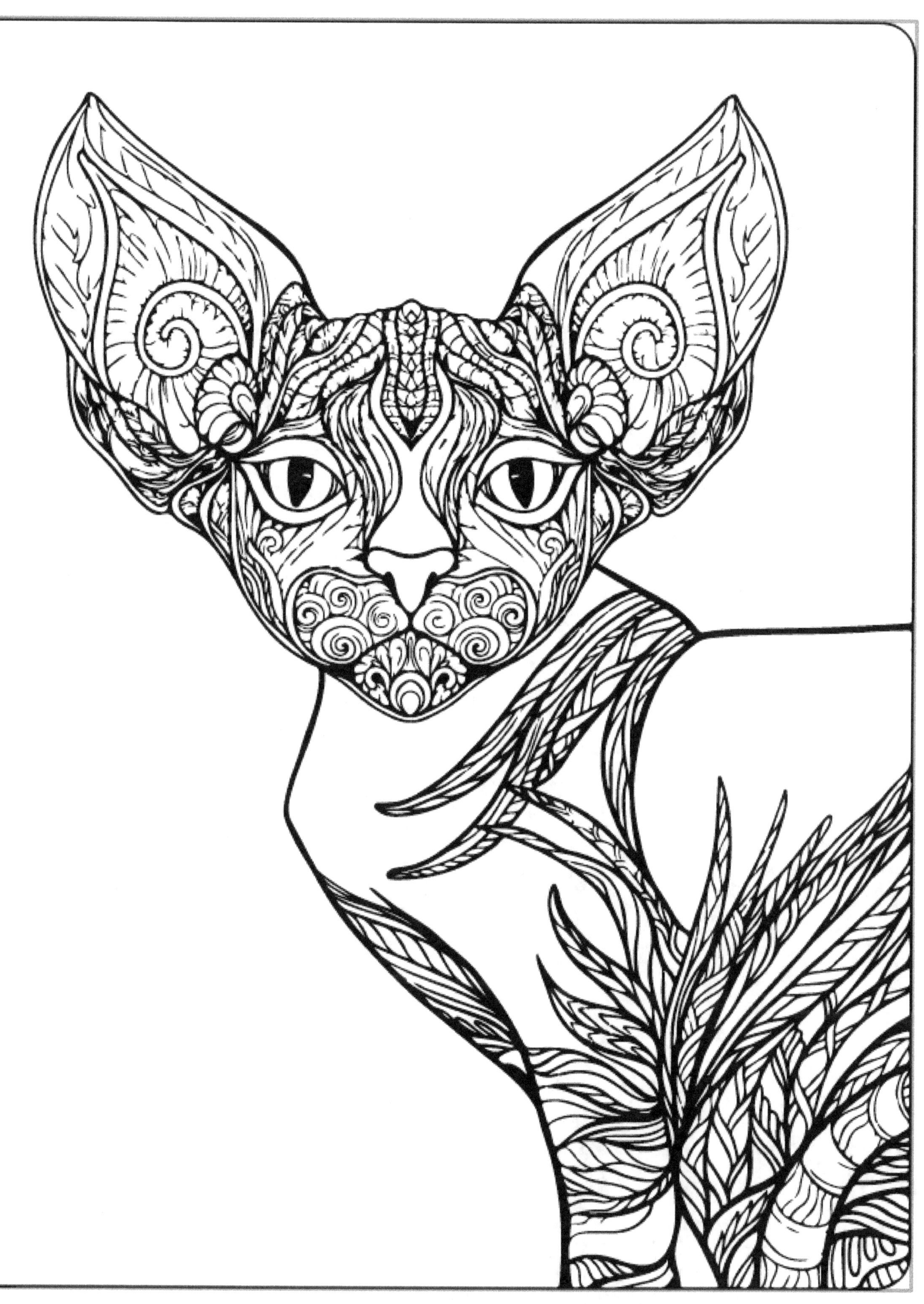

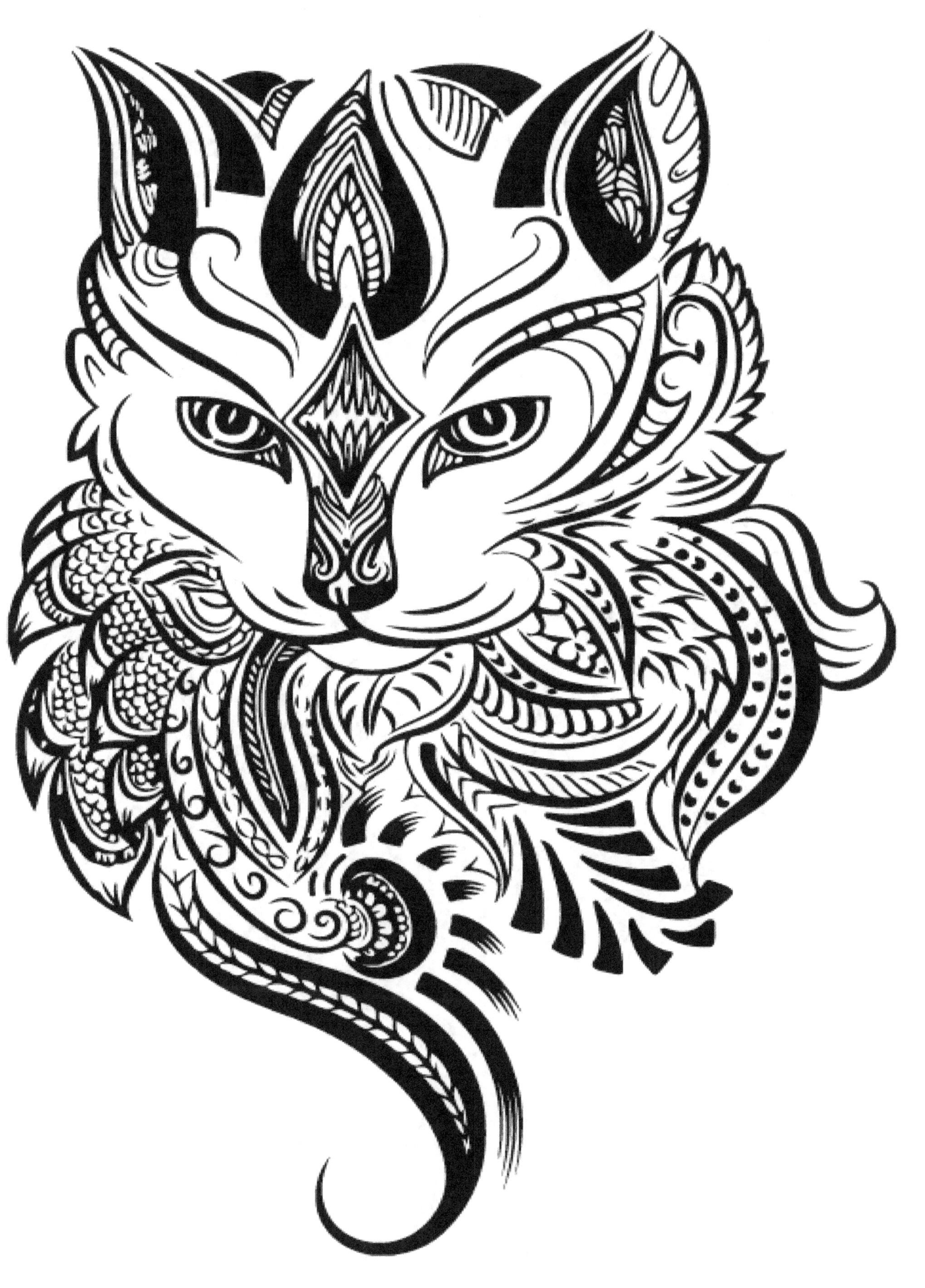

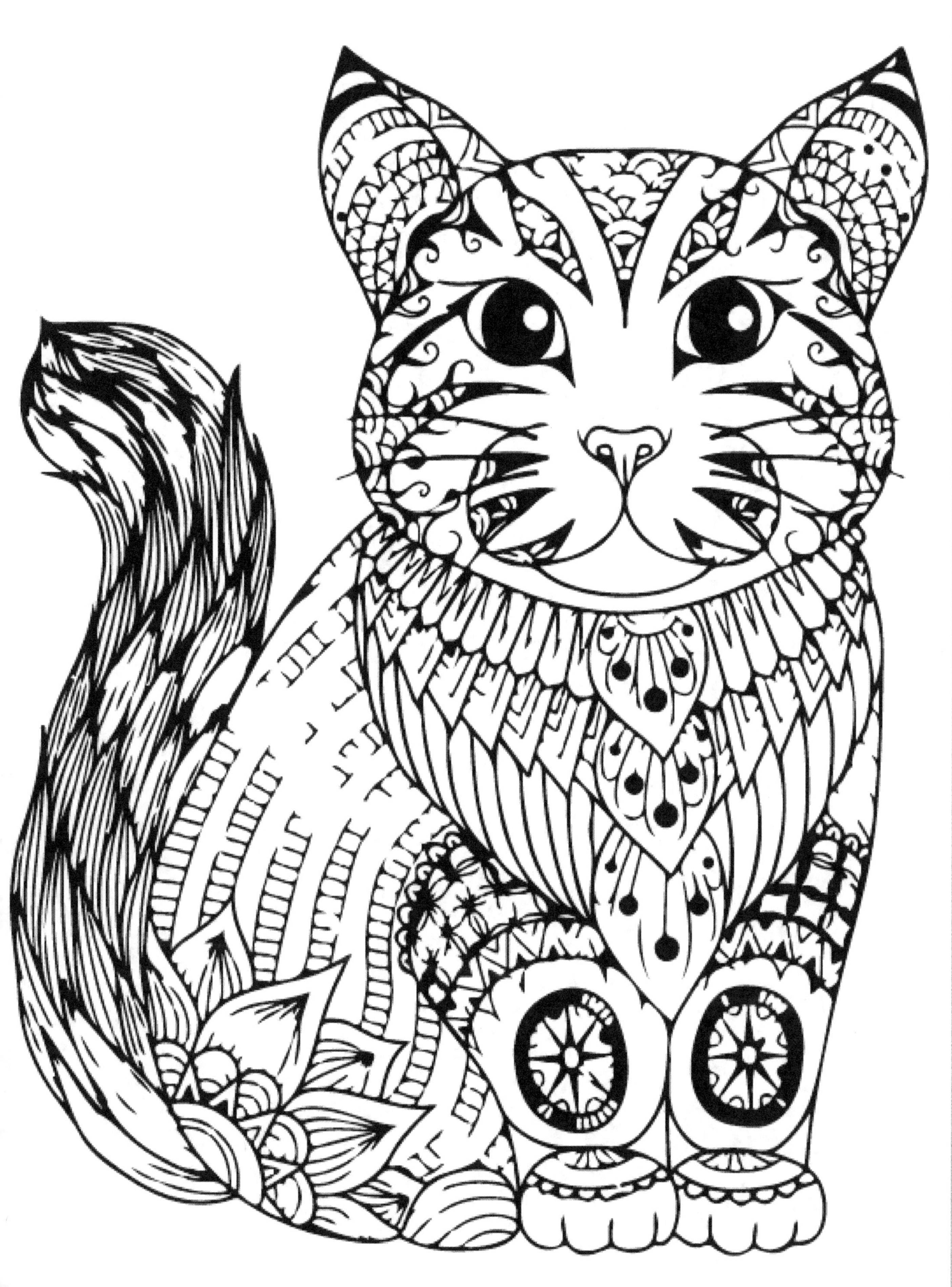

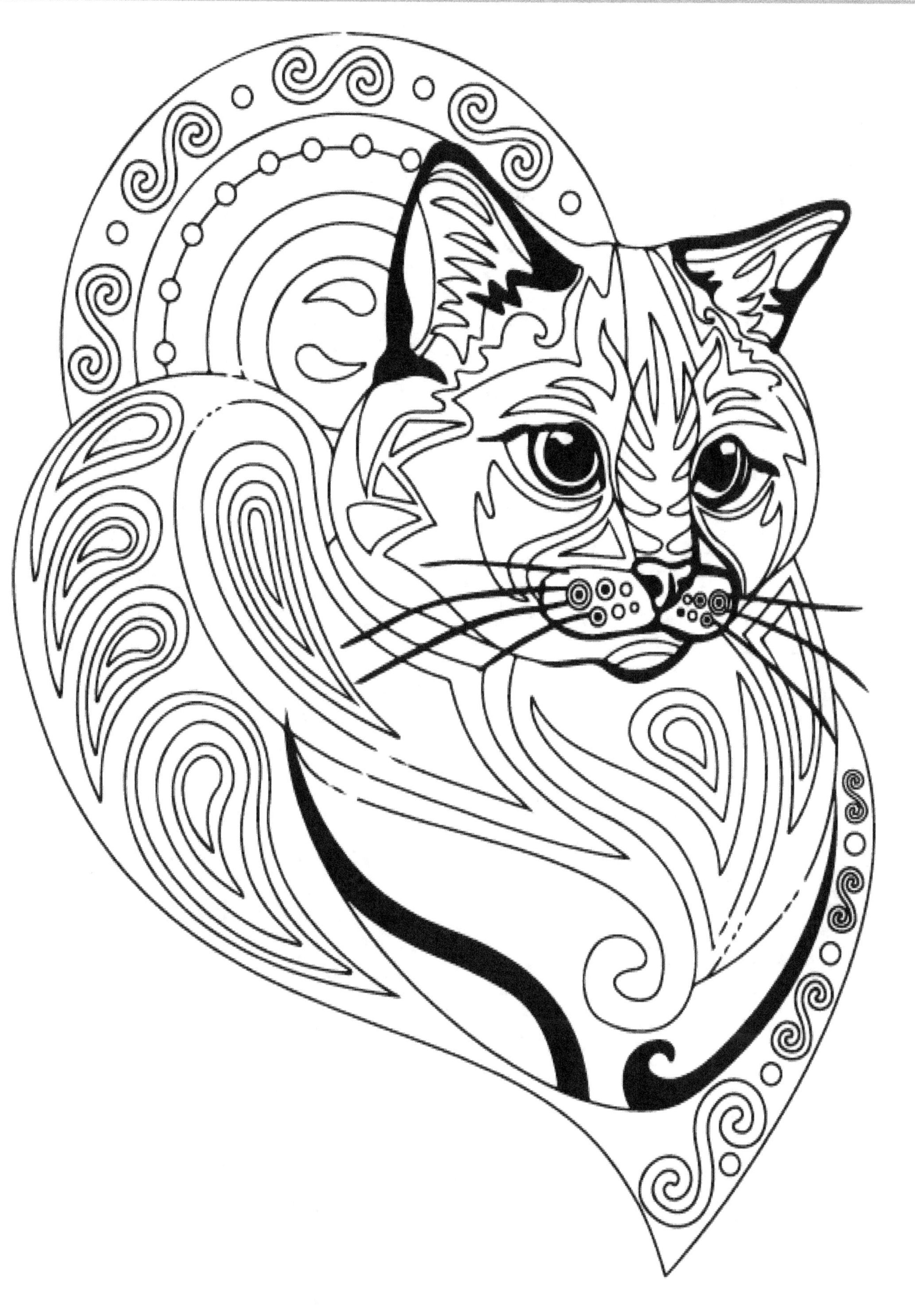

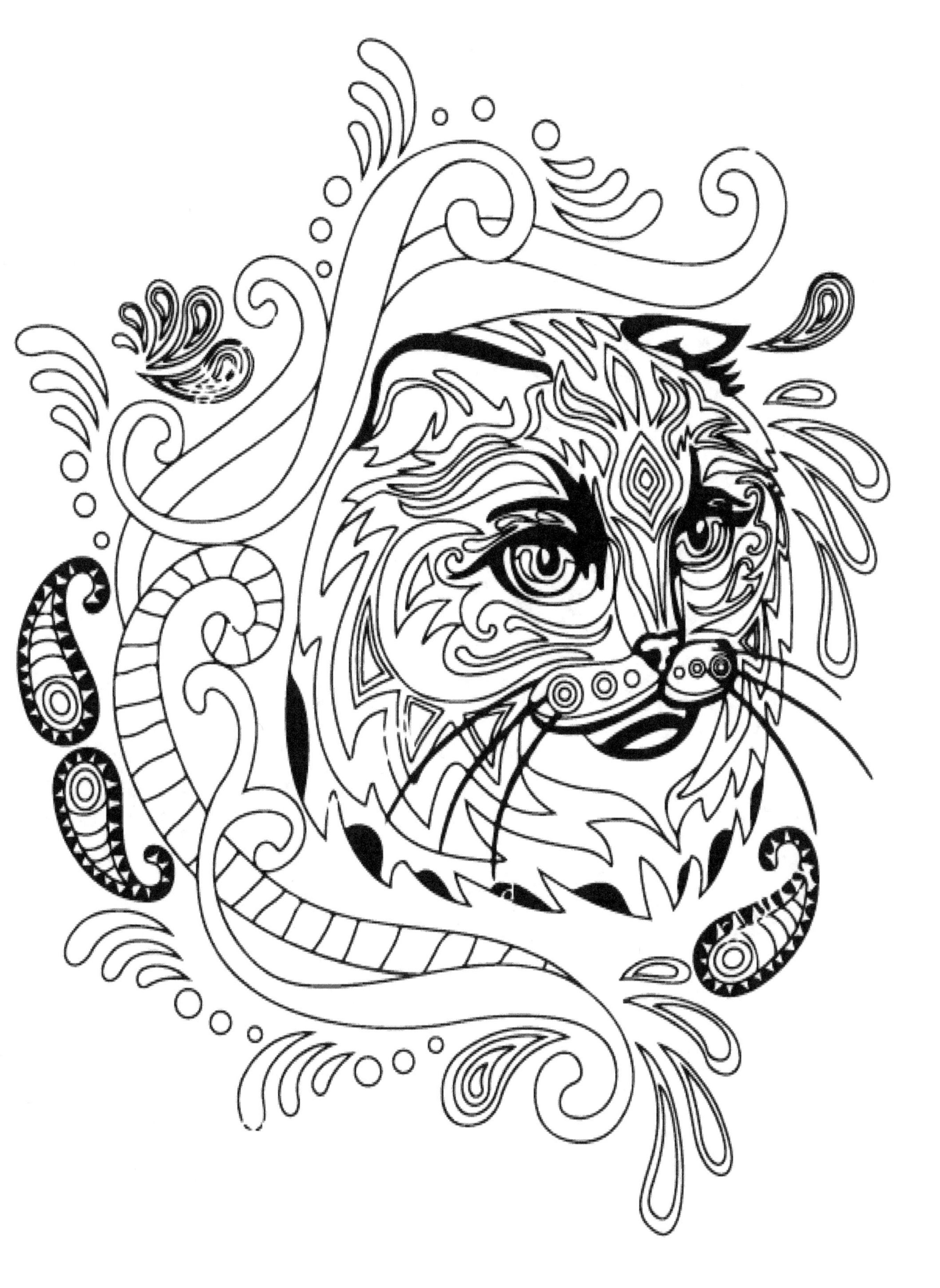

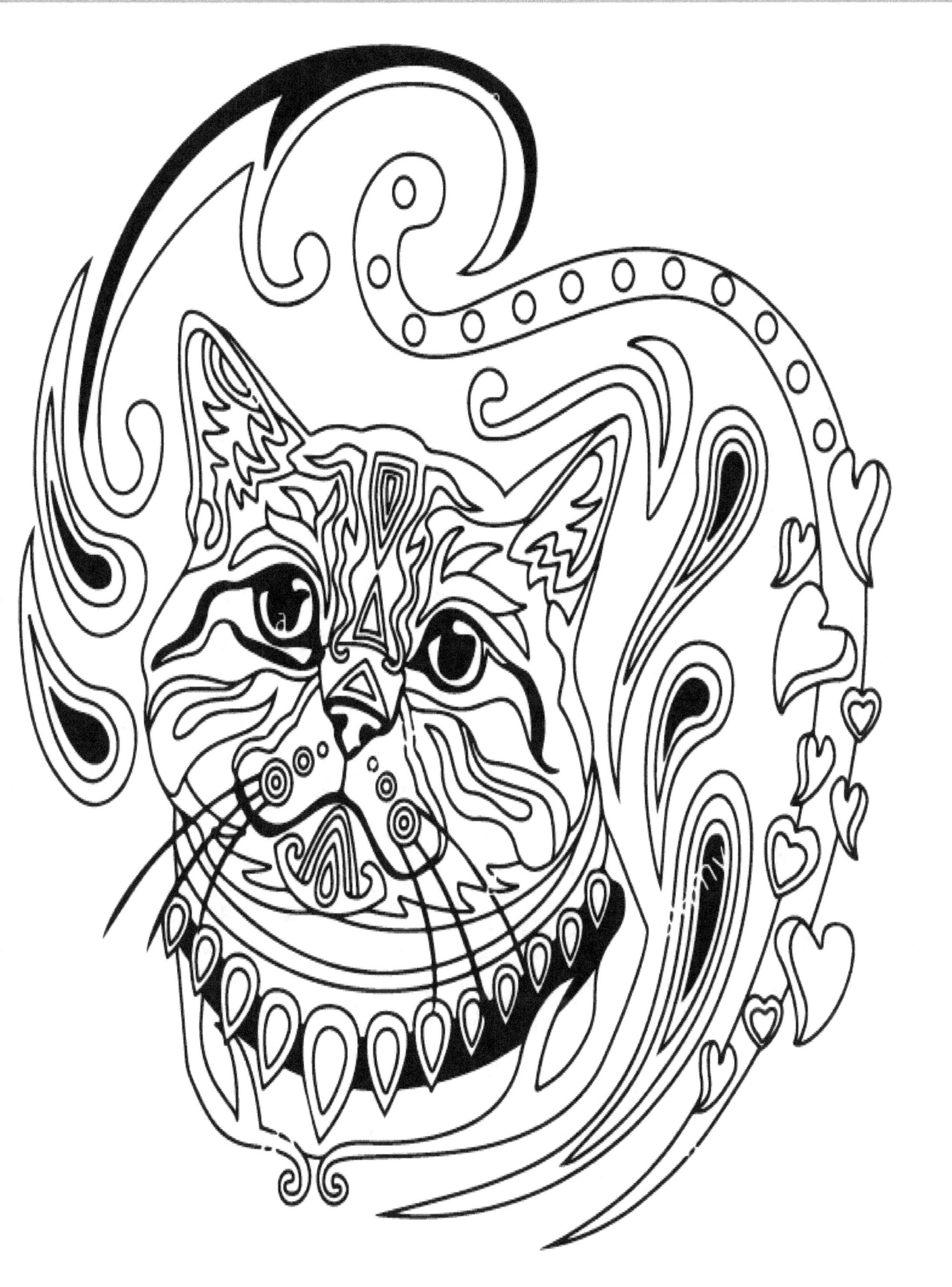

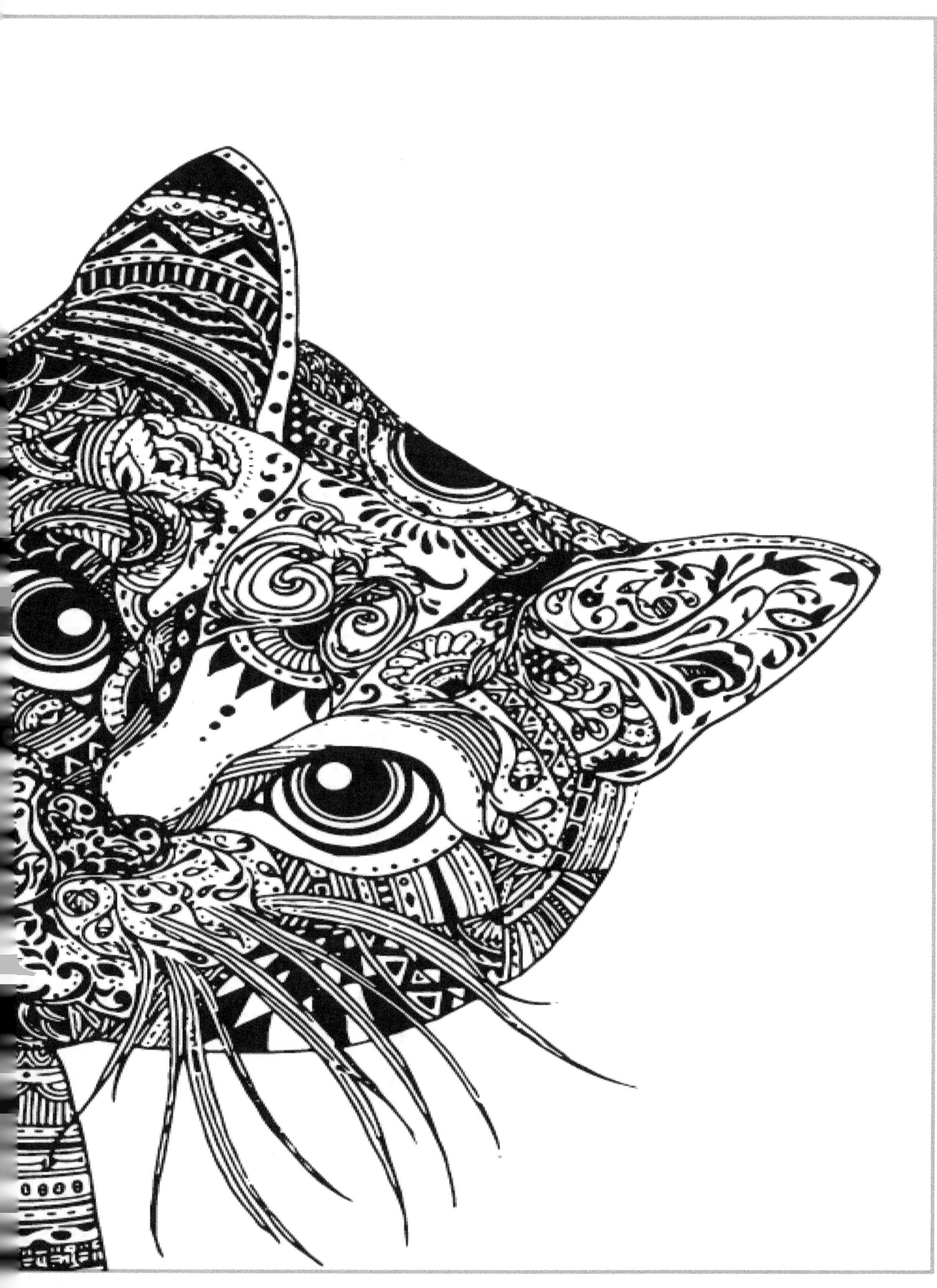

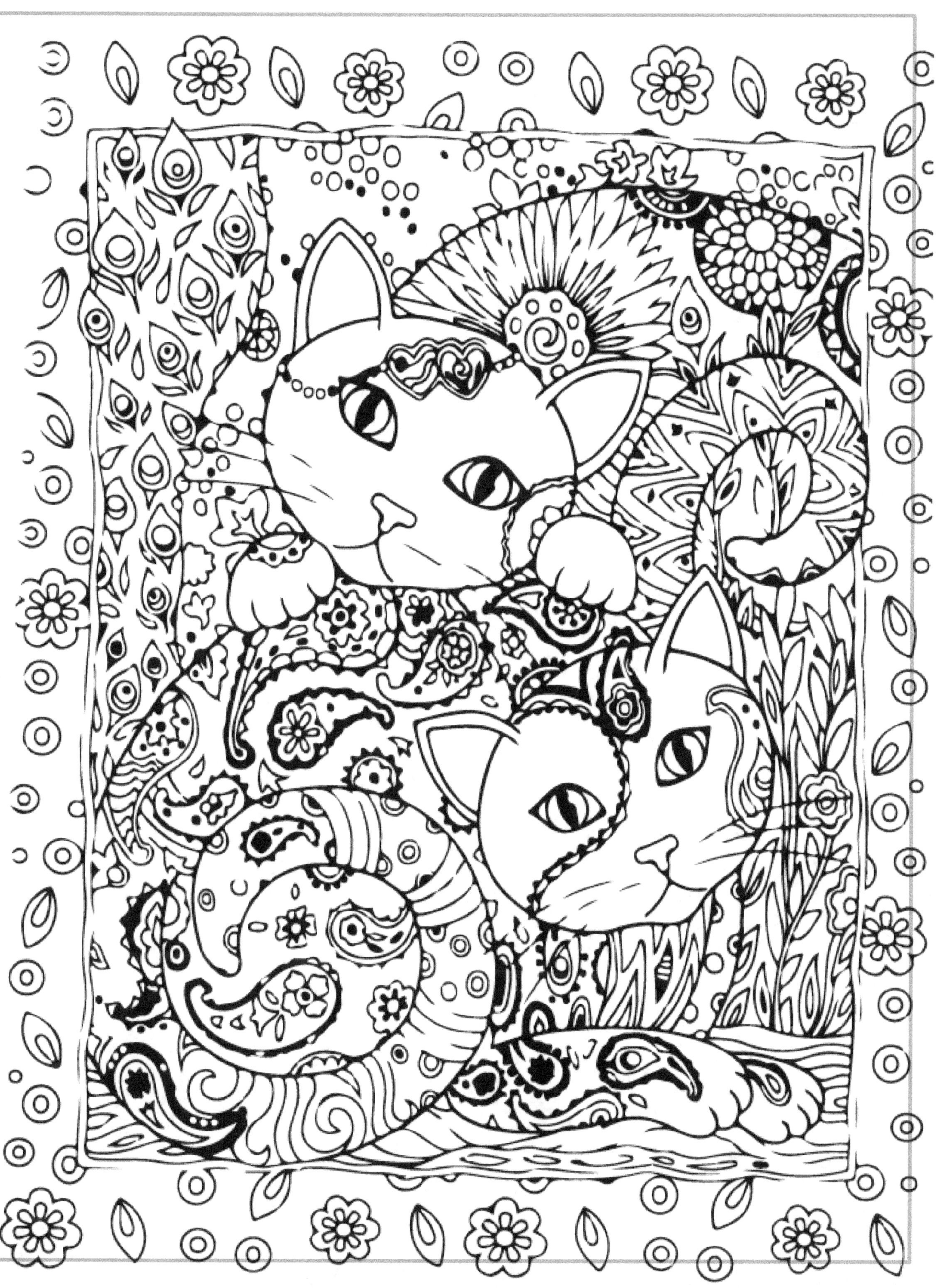

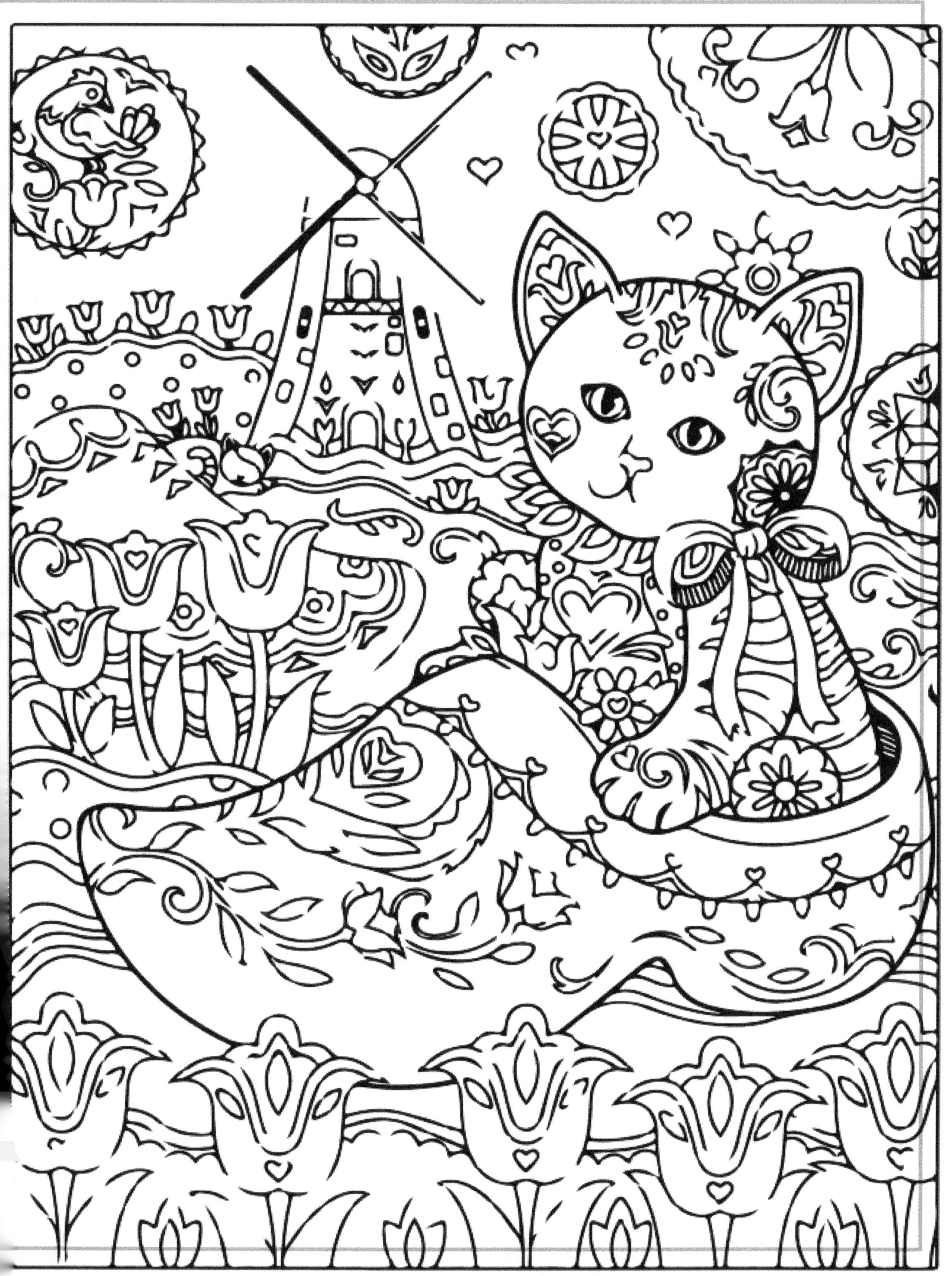

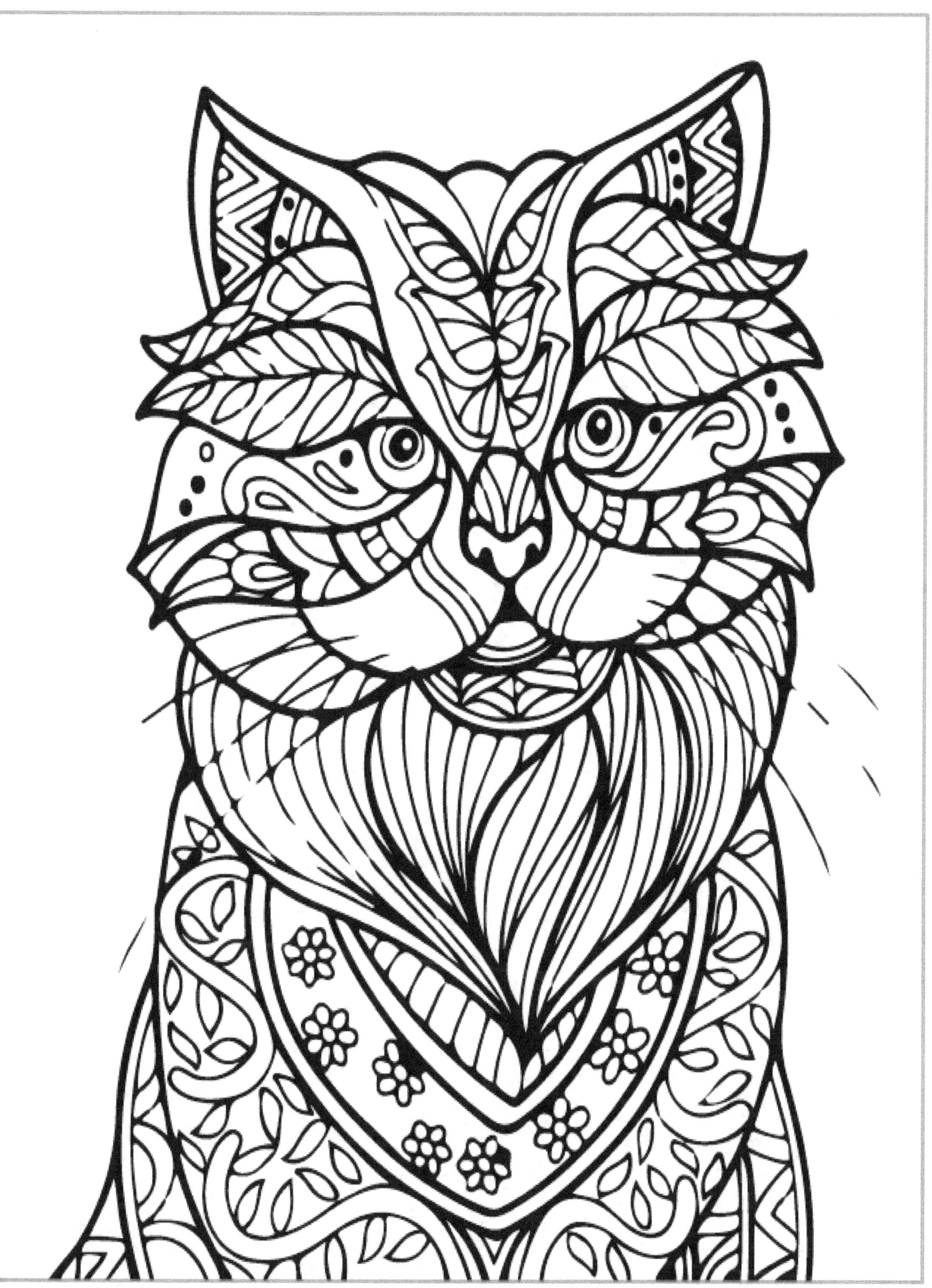

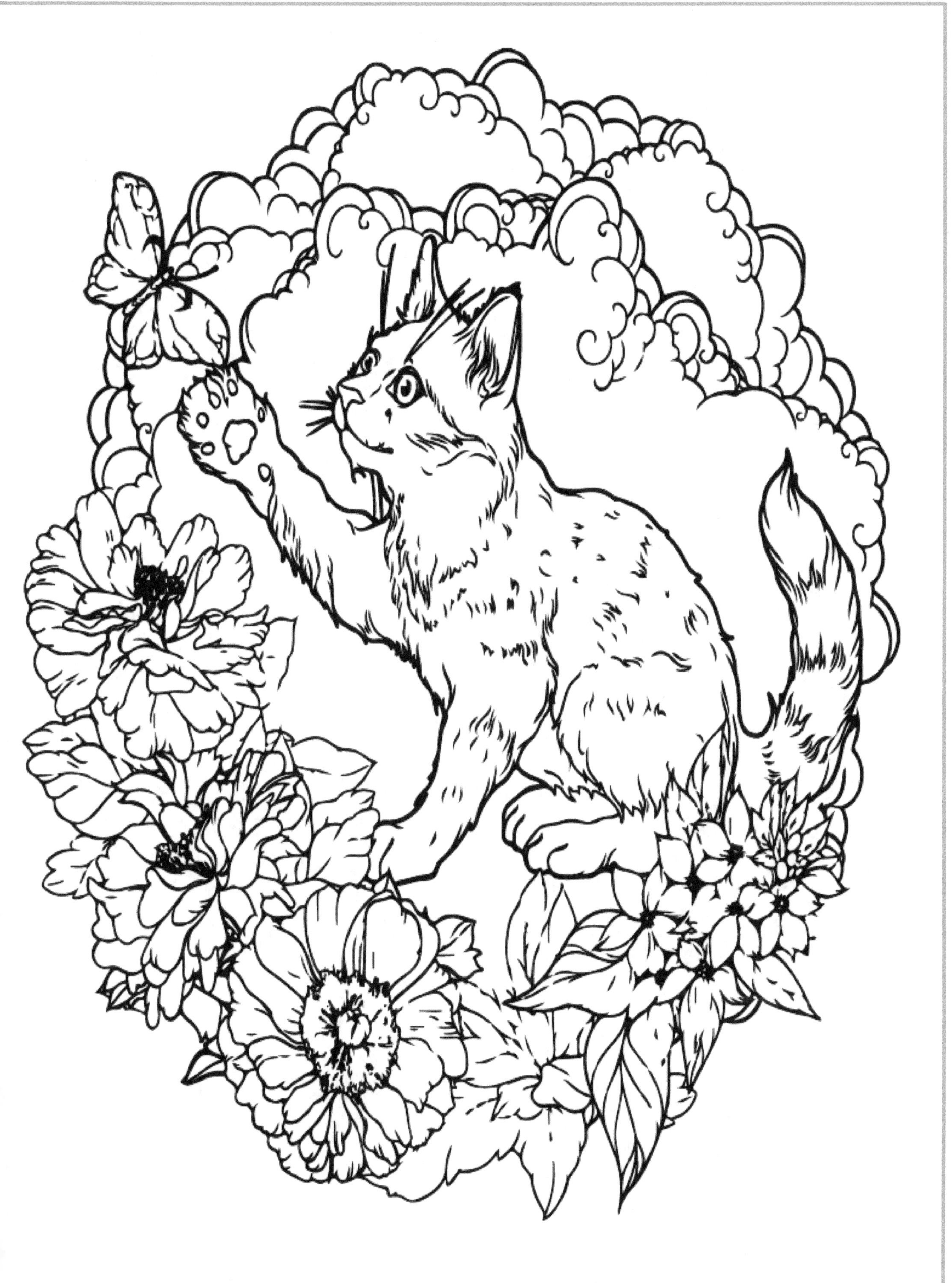

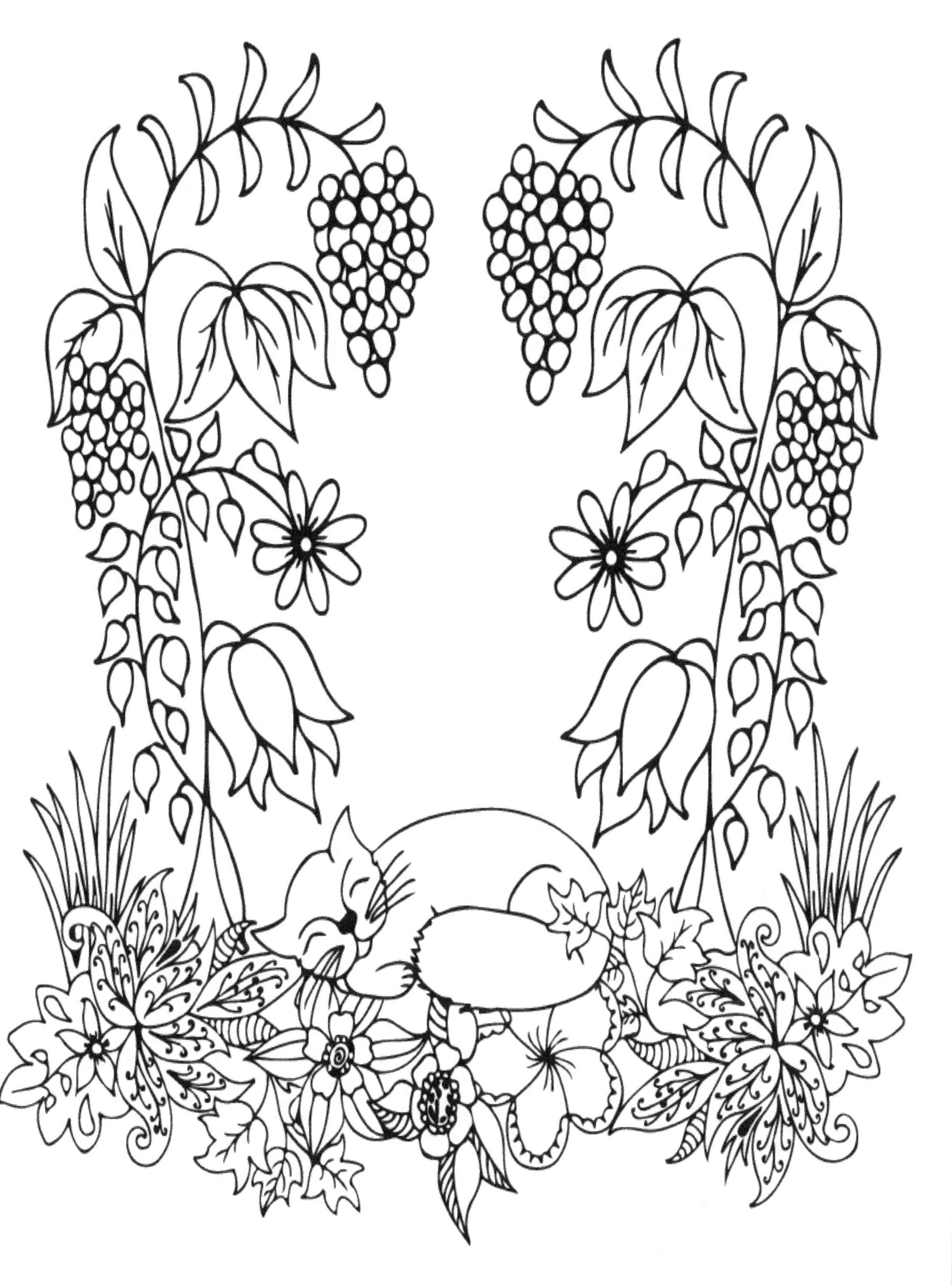

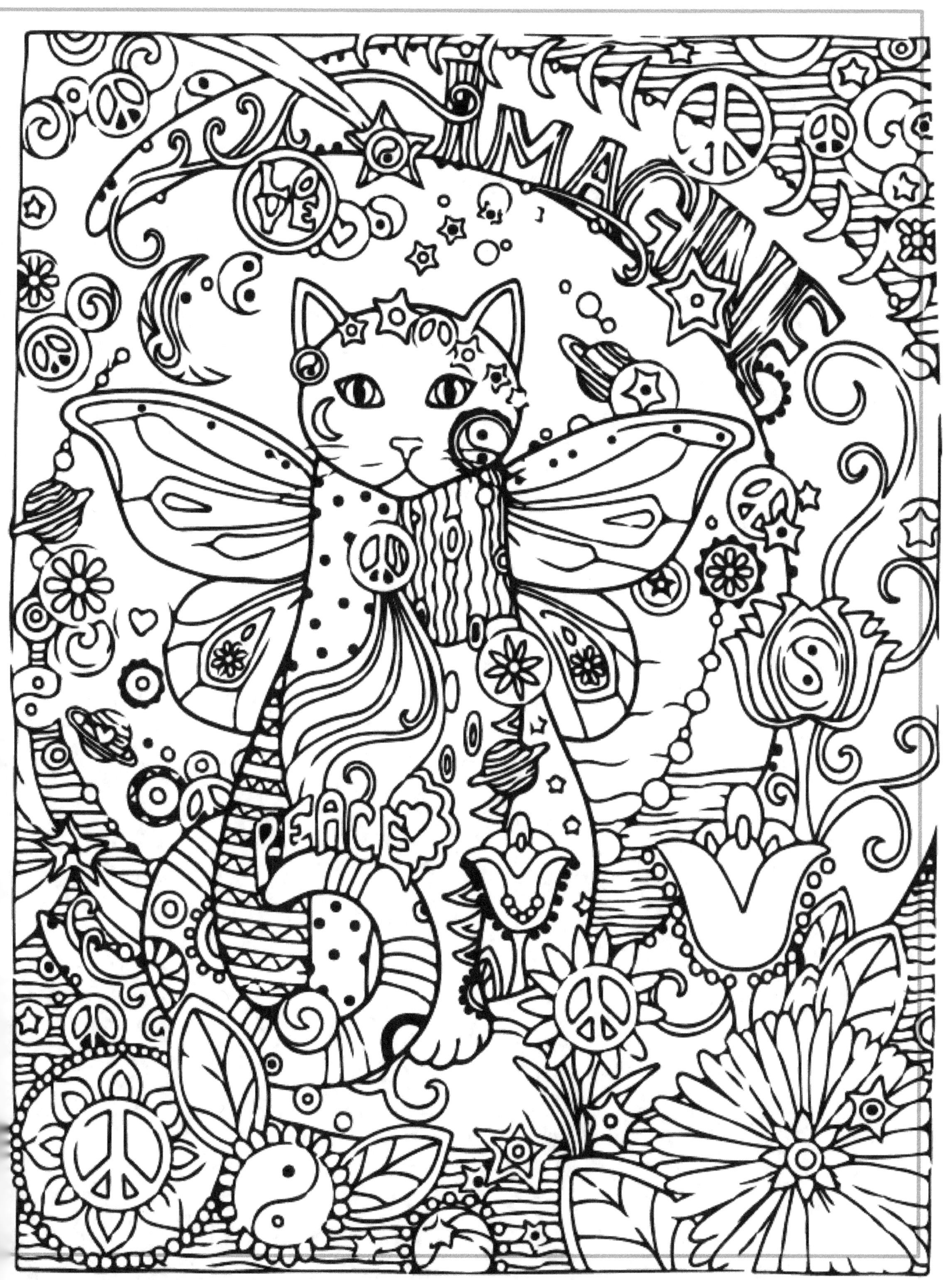

IMAGINE
LOVE
PEACE

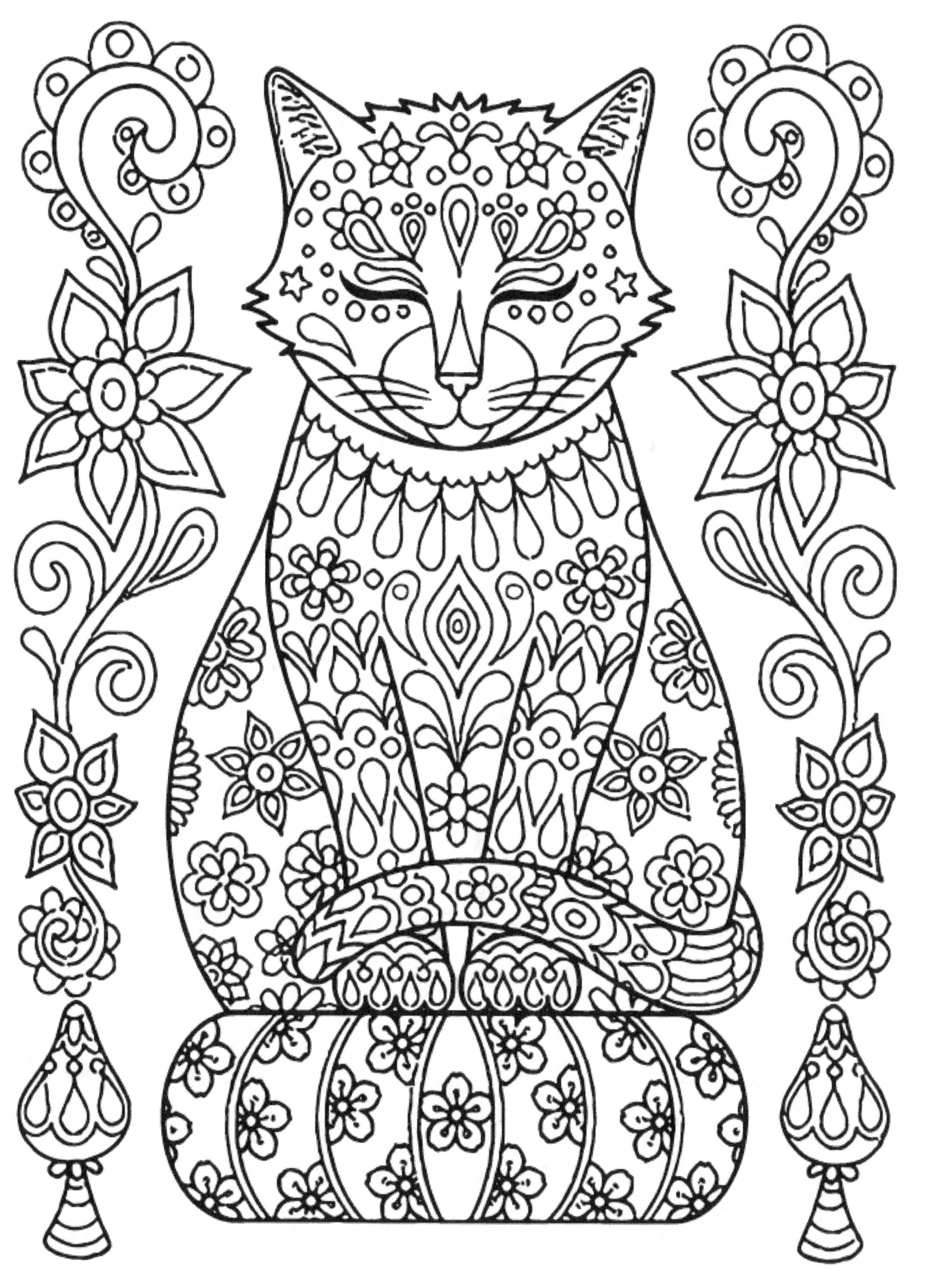

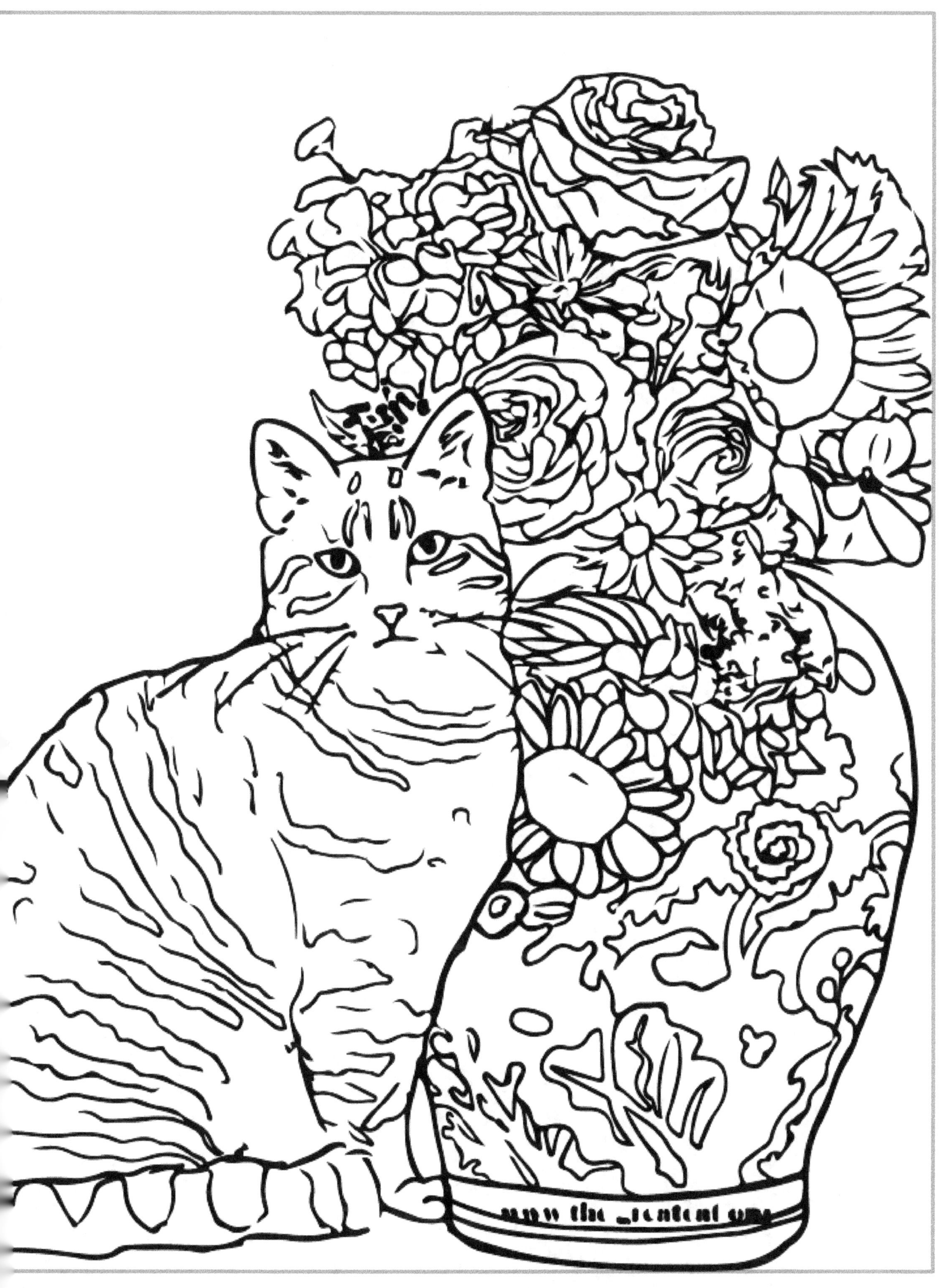

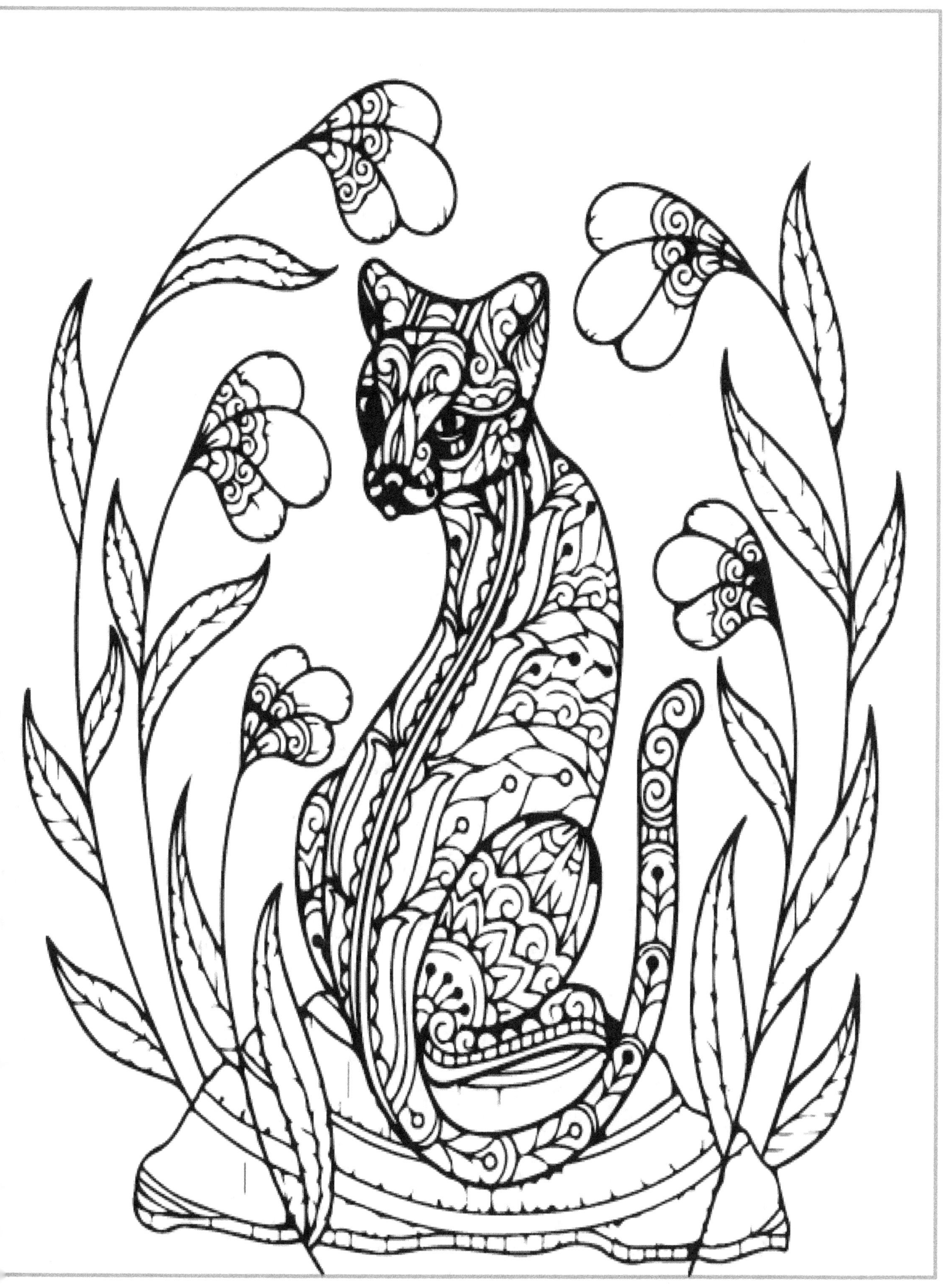

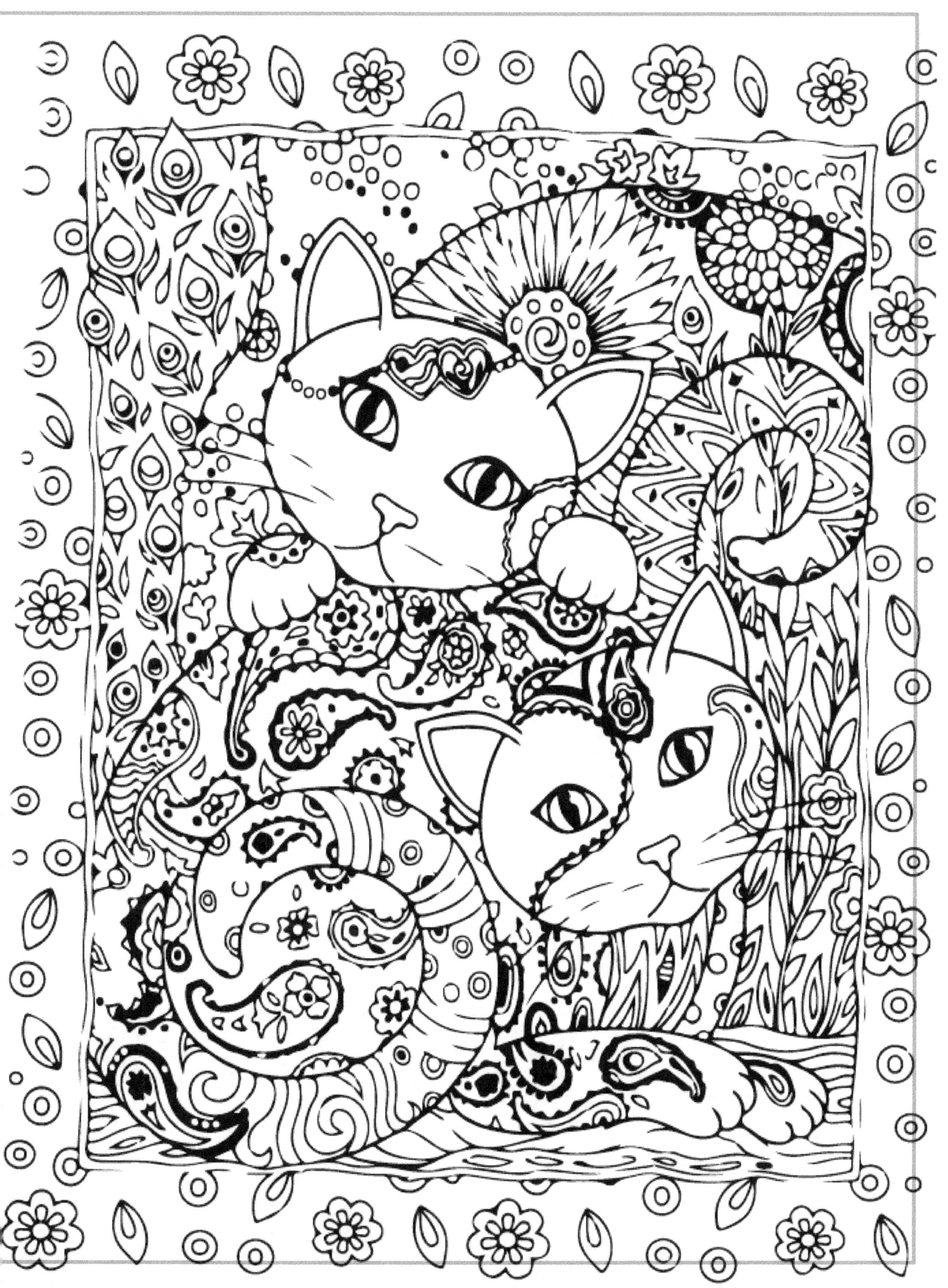

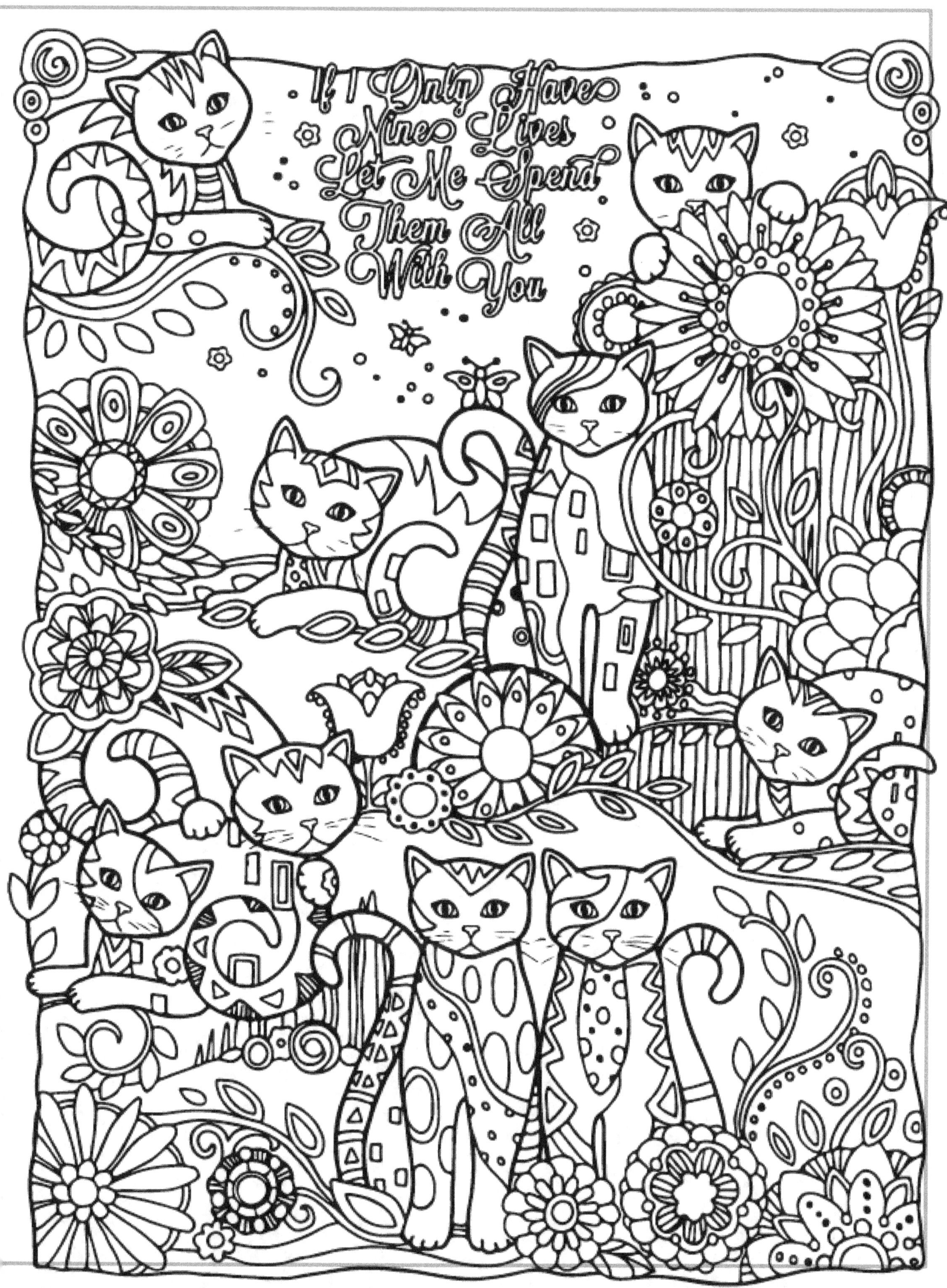

If I Only Have
Nine Lives
Let Me Spend
Them All
With You

www.ingramcontent.com/pod-product-compliance
Lightning Source LLC
Chambersburg PA
CBHW081400160726
48000CB00010B/3419